Being MENTORED

With profound admiration and respect, I dedicate this book
to the men and women who have chosen to
dedicate themselves to honing the intellect and empowering
the creativity of their protégés: today's youth. It is you,
serving as both mentors and teachers to your students,
who pave the path to the future.

Being MENTORED

A GUIDE FOR PROTÉGÉS

HAL PORTNER

CORWIN PRESS, INC.
A Sage Publications Company
Thousand Oaks, California

For information:

 Corwin Press, Inc.
A Sage Publications Company
2455 Teller Road
Thousand Oaks, California 91320
www.corwinpress.com

Sage Publications Ltd.
6 Bonhill Street
London EC2A 4PU
United Kingdom

Sage Publications India Pvt. Ltd.
M-32 Market
Greater Kailash I
New Delhi 110 048 India

Printed in the United States of America

Library of Congress Cataloging-in-Publication Data

Portner, Hal.
 Being mentored: A guide for proteges / by Hal Portner.
    p. cm.
 Includes bibliographical references and index.
  ISBN 978-0-7619-4552-9 (c: acid-free paper)
  ISBN 978-0-7619-4553-6 (p: acid-free paper)
  1. Mentoring in education—United States. 2. First-year teachers—United States. 3. Teachers—In-service training—United States. I. Title.
  LB1731.4 .P65 2002
  371.1—dc21

                                        2002005699

This book is printed on acid-free paper.

07 08 09 10 9 8 7 6 5

Acquisitions Editor:	Robb Clouse
Editorial Assistant:	Erin Buchanan
Copy Editor:	Elisabeth Magnus
Production Editor:	Denise Santoyo
Typesetter:	Siva Math Setters, Chennai, India
Cover Designer:	Tracy E. Miller
Production Artist:	Sandra Ng

Contents

Preface

Over the next 10 years in the United States alone, more than 2 million new teachers are expected to enter the profession. Every one of these beginners will have two jobs: (a) to teach and (b) to learn to teach better.

To help new teachers "learn to teach better," most states in the United States require that every new teacher be matched with a trained mentor. In response to the challenge imposed by mandates to provide support for beginning teachers and in recognition of the promise mentoring holds as a vehicle for educational reform, increasing numbers of school districts have arranged for experienced teachers to help their new colleagues persevere and develop beyond their difficult first years.

Even with the support of a dedicated and knowledgeable mentor, a new teacher may not always be willing or able to get the most out of being mentored. To benefit fully from the experience, the teacher needs to be willing and able to seize opportunities when they are available and to create them when they are not. That is what this book is about.

WHO SHOULD READ THIS BOOK

Being Mentored: A Guide for Protégés is written for the potential teacher, the student teacher, and the new teacher who has, expects to have, is required to have, or hopes to have an experienced educator as a cooperating teacher or mentor. The book is intended as (a) a reference and workbook for the practicing or prospective new teacher; (b) a source book for both individuals and groups of participants in student teaching or practicum programs; (c) a practical resource for mentors, mentoring program coordinators, and mentoring committee members; and (d) a resource to include along with other orientation material for new teachers.

Experienced teachers new to a school or district should find many of the guide's principles applicable to their situations, as will educators at practically any point in their careers.

OVERVIEW OF THE CONTENTS

Being Mentored: A Guide for Protégés contains thought-provoking activities and discussions of the essential skills, understandings, and behaviors needed to profit from being a recipient in the mentoring process. Each chapter provides a set of principles for success and offers suggestions for action. Also featured is an annotated compendium of publications and Internet sites of special interest to new teachers.

The introduction tells a little about the mentoring process and presents an overview of what it means to be a proactive protégé.

Chapter 1, "Participate," answers the question: How can protégés contribute to the development and maintenance of mentoring relationships?

Chapter 2, "Take Responsibility," answers the question: How can protégés take responsibility and be proactive in the mentoring process?

Chapter 3, "Observe," answers the question: How can protégés take advantage of opportunities to observe others teach?

Chapter 4, "Ask," answers the question: How can protégés solicit and receive help?

Chapter 5, "Chart Your Course," answers the question: How can protégés identify what they need to know and make decisions about their own professional development?

Chapter 6, "Network," answers the question: How can protégés seek out and create opportunities to exchange information and support with their peers?

Chapter 7, "Take Informed Risks," answers the question: How can protégés learn by trying something new or doing something differently?

Chapter 8, "Reflect," answers the question: How can protégés critically examine the implications of their experiences in order to learn?

Chapter 9, "Give Back," answers the question: How can protégés contribute to their schools' programs, procedures, and culture?

Resource A, "Internet Sites and Publications for New Teachers," presents an annotated selection of print and electronic materials that a new teacher may find useful.

Resource B, "Professional Organizations and Their Web Pages," provides a representative list of subject-specific associations and their Web page addresses.

Resource C, "Chatboard Exchange on the Internet," is a verbatim request for help from beginning teachers posed by a mentor-teacher and the set of responses she received over the ensuing 24 hours.

Acknowledgments

My profound thanks goes to the many teachers, professors, and student-interns whose comments, experiences, and reflections—some related during conversations, several recounted in publications, and others posted on Internet chatboards—were the major impetus for writing this book.

Following are the full names of some of these individuals. Only a first name or some other descriptor was provided by additional people, and several more (they know who they are) prefer to remain anonymous:

Cathy Foltz, Phu N. Ly, Christopher Markofski, Michael Massailo, Patricia A. Jones, Jennifer Powers, Melanie Pritchard, Lisa Rock, Judith Smith, Lonna H. Smith, Cheryl, kwajmoon, Michelle J., Spineless, DJ, Jane, Jill S., A. Sills, Bitsy, Margaret M., Jeannette W., Ilene L., Melanie P., Julie, Judith S., Lisa R., Sharon, Jennifer, Gwen, Dan L., Betty S., Jamie, Emma, Kris, Rosa, Margaret M., and Ken R.

I am indebted to you all. You have my deep appreciation for your willingness to share and my utmost admiration for your insights, suggestions, and dedication to the profession.

I especially want to thank Robert Pauker, consultant and long-time associate; Janine Lapan, a second-year teacher; Jennifer Seydel, a teacher-education professor and student teacher advisor at Springfield (Mass.) College; and the knowledgeable peer reviewers selected by Corwin Press to be my critical friends. These colleagues have graciously reviewed drafts of the book's manuscript. Many of their perceptive comments and thoughtful suggestions have been incorporated into this book.

I am fortunate to have had the opportunity of having Corwin Press's Robb Clouse and Elisabeth Magnus as my editors. Their professionalism, encouragement, and flexibility, along with the timely cooperation of Robb's coworkers, are much appreciated.

Most especially, I admire, respect, and am indebted to my wife, Mary, who decided, after several successful years working in the private sector as a graphic designer, to change careers, go to graduate school, work as an Americorps volunteer with adjudicated youth in an inner-city school, and become a teacher. She has been not only my cheerleader while I was writing this book but also my sentinel in terms of the book's relation to reality.

About the Author

 **Hal Portner** is a former K-12 teacher and administrator. He was Assistant Director of the SummerMath Program for High School Women and their Teachers at Mount Holyoke College, and for 24 years he was a teacher and then administrator in two Connecticut public school districts. He holds an MEd from the University of Michigan and a 6th-year Certificate of Advanced Graduate Study in education administration from the University of Connecticut. For 3 years, he was with the University of Massachusetts EdD Educational Leadership Program. From 1985 to 1995, he was on the staff of the Connecticut State Department of Education's Bureau of Certification and Professional Development, where, among other responsibilities, he served as Coordinator of the Connecticut Institute for Teaching and Learning and worked closely with school districts to develop and carry out professional development and teacher evaluation plans and programs. He writes, develops materials, trains mentors, facilitates the development of new-teacher and peer-mentoring programs, and consults for school districts and other educational organizations and institutions. He is the author of *Mentoring New Teachers* (1998, 2002), and *Training Mentors Is Not Enough: Everything Else Schools and Districts Need to Do* (2001).

Introduction

Teachers open the door, but you must enter by yourself.

Chinese proverb

I have spent quite a few years serving as a mentor to others and being mentored by others. I am a consultant to mentoring programs. I train mentors. I write about mentoring. I read what others write about mentoring. Above all, I listen to what protégés and their mentors say about their mentoring experiences. All of these encounters have given me the unique opportunity to interact with many student teachers and new teachers and to learn from them how they view mentoring and to what extent they participate in the mentoring process. This book is a summation of what I have learned. It is written for those of you who recently have been hired—or expect soon to be hired—as a first-year teacher.

If you are such an individual, congratulations! You have entered—or are about to enter—one of the world's noblest, most gratifying professions. How does it feel? Exhilarating and inspiring? Confusing and scary? Perhaps a little of each or somewhere in between?

Like you, the millions of people who will be hired as first-time educators over the next 10 years will experience such a range of feelings—especially when they realize that "new teachers have two jobs to do—they have to teach and they have to learn to teach [better]" (Wildman, Niles, Magliaro, & McLaughlin, 1989, p. 471).

"What?" you might ask. "Learn to teach better? I have already spent a lot of time and energy—not to mention money—and

1

earned lots of college credits learning how to teach. Now you want me to . . ."

Okay, okay, calm down. Feelings of elation or trepidation aside, you probably do consider yourself prepared to tackle job one: to teach. You presumably have acquired considerable expertise from your most recent college experience, including in-depth knowledge about a particular subject and an extensive repertoire of instructional theories. In fact, although you may be a novice in the teaching profession, you may actually know as much about some of the latest developments in these areas as some experienced teachers do—possibly even more.

However, before you sit back complacently, consider this:

> A college degree in education only takes you so far. It prepares you to become a beginner in a complex world. What expert teachers have is case knowledge. They can go back in their memory banks to compare situations and figure out what to do. . . . They know [from references stored in their memory] how to get from point A to point B. Novices have no such [stored] experiences. (Scherer, 2001, p. 6)

Understand, too, that years of experience alone are not enough. Alas, although I have been a painter for years, I am not a Rembrandt. Successful teaching is an art that takes insight and knowledge, in addition to time, to develop. Unfortunately, there are all too many instances where new teachers do not remain in the profession long enough to develop the art of teaching or where they stay but merely settle for adequacy.

One reason for a high attrition rate and less-than-exemplary effectiveness is that, typically, new teachers have not had, or did not take advantage of, initial or ongoing support. They were literally isolated—or they isolated themselves—behind classroom doors with little feedback or help. According to the September 1996 report of the National Commission on Teaching and America's Future, the evidence is clear: "Supports for new teachers help them continue their learning during a critical period, one which makes a tremendous difference in the kind of teacher they become and the kind of experience their students have" (p. 82). In other words, without appropriate assistance and encouragement, many new teachers are unable to do their second job: learn to teach better.

Recently, more and more educational policymakers and leaders have come to recognize that mentoring is a powerful and effective way to help new teachers learn to teach. Most states have mandated some form of mentoring support and assistance for beginning teachers. Both the National Education Association and the American Federation of Teachers, the nation's largest teachers' unions, are in accord in their encouragement of the establishment of programs under which all beginning teachers would be assigned a mentor. Increasing numbers of school districts have arranged for experienced teachers to help their new colleagues persist and develop beyond their difficult first year.

Are you fulfilling a college or university teacher-preparation program's practicum/student teaching requirement? Have you been recently hired, or do you expect soon to be hired, as a first-year teacher? If so, you may already have, or you soon will have, the opportunity to be the protégé of a teacher-mentor.

Are you ready, willing, and able to take advantage of being mentored? If you have or soon will have the degree and certification that make you eligible for a teaching position in a public school, you are probably ready to teach. The fact that you are reading this also indicates that you may be ready to put some effort into working with a mentor on "job two," learning to teach better.

Even if you are ready to be mentored, you may not get as much out of the experience as you would if you were also willing. Are you willing to take the responsibility—to put in the extra time and effort that learning to teach better will take? Being willing to get as much as you can from being mentored means the following:

1. You believe that you have an ongoing need to learn to teach better. When you are doing something you believe in— when what you are doing sits well with your set of values and is relevant to your life—you will do it better; you will do it with passion.

2. You have confidence that being mentored can help you learn to teach better—that mentoring can make a difference between success and failure in the classroom. You understand not only that mentoring can contribute to a smooth transition from campus to classroom but that it also provides the opportunity to receive the kind of feedback and guidance that can shorten the time it will take you to become a master teacher.

3. You truly want to be the best teacher you can be. Being mentored can help you remain in the profession and have a successful and gratifying career. Patricia A. Jones, Assistant Principal of the Point Pleasant Elementary School in Glen Burnie, Maryland, told me recently that after her district instituted a mentoring program, the percentage of new teachers leaving after a year or two fell from 18% to 2%.

Finally, are you *able* to get the most out of being mentored? Whether you have a mentor who offers little or no help or support or a mentor who throws so much information and help your way that you are constantly overwhelmed, or even if you have the good fortune to have as a mentor an experienced teacher who understands how to work effectively with a protégé, you will still get more out of being mentored if you are able. Being able means having the knowledge, skills, and understandings necessary to be proactive in the mentoring process. Being proactive means not only being ready and willing to access the resources available to you but also being empowered to do so.

That is the purpose of this book: to empower you with the skills, knowledge, and understandings that will help you get the most out of being mentored.

CHAPTER ONE

Participate

It takes two to tango.

Anonymous

Jane, a mentor-teacher with 8 years of classroom experience, told me recently about her experience with one of her protégés. "The guy I am mentoring," she sighed, "rarely seeks me out. When we do get to talk, I get the feeling he isn't much interested. To top it off, I was told he referred to me as 'the company spy' in front of others in the copy room. What bothers me most, however, is that he has acquired some good teaching skills in college and I feel that I can help him effectively apply them—but I'm beginning to think it's not worth the effort."

What a tragedy! Jane's protégé may never have the opportunity to get any productive mentoring out of her simply because he failed to realize that (a) mentoring takes place within a working relationship and (b) the development of a working relationship requires the active participation of both its parties.

Mentoring takes place within a working relationship, and the development of a working relationship requires the active participation of both its parties.

TAKE THE INITIATIVE

So what can you do as a new teacher to share in the development of a productive mentoring relationship? Luckner and Nadler

5

(1997) postulated that "individuals need to build and maintain rapport throughout a relationship. . . . The key to building rapport is to make others feel accepted, supported, and comfortable" (pp. 76-77). They go on to suggest some general strategies that tend to communicate acceptance: (a) Use the person's name; (b) maintain eye contact; (c) appear calm, yet energized; (d) use effective communication skills—listen actively, paraphrase, summarize, clarify, and ask for more detail; (e) give credit to individuals for their ideas and accomplishments; (f) refrain from making judgments; and (g) offer information about yourself when appropriate.

In many instances, new teachers won't meet their mentors until the first day of teacher orientation. Don't wait until then. If at all possible, find out before the school year begins who your mentor will be and how to contact her or him. Introduce yourself. Arrange to meet. If you do have the opportunity to meet and have no particular agenda other than to get acquainted, then let the conversation take its own course.

On the other hand, there may be situations where this initial meeting does need to be more focused. For example, last summer Jill S. posted a message on an Internet chatboard. "My mentor," she wrote, "is going to be someone that is a very close friend of the family. I respect her very much and really couldn't ask for a better mentor . . . except that I can't help feeling that she is the adult and that I am the little girl in pigtails once again. . . . She's not going to see me as an adult! I'm a little worried and concerned about how it will work out."

This was my response. "Worried and concerned, Jill? Sure you are. But you have a good chance of nipping those feelings in the bud if you sit down with your friend/mentor before school starts and have a heart-to-heart talk during which you express your feelings and ask for hers. This is also a good time to discuss expectations and for you to let her know that you are looking forward to working together as colleagues and to the opportunity of being inducted into the profession by a knowledgeable friend and mentor."

DEVELOPING THE RELATIONSHIP TAKES TIME

Building a solid mentoring relationship doesn't happen overnight, nor does it always happen smoothly. Scholtes (1988) identified four stages of group development that apply equally to the stages you can expect your developing relationship with your mentor to take over time. Going through these stages is a normal function of building a mentor-protégé relationship. Understanding and honoring them will help you work through whatever difficulties you might encounter. The stages are

1. *Forming.* This is the stage in which you and your mentor cautiously explore boundaries and begin to build trust. It is characterized by excitement, anticipation, and anxiety about what lies ahead. Attempts are made to define the task at hand, and discussions tend to be both problem oriented and about general topics. Little may be accomplished in terms of tasks or goals; the focus, rather, is on developing rapport.

2. *Storming.* This is the most difficult stage. This is when you may become defensive and question the wisdom of your mentor. You may become impatient, tense, or indecisive with any lack of progress.

3. *Norming.* During this stage, you and your mentor will have reconciled any differences and will be able to express any concerns constructively. Trust and collaboration are evident, and a friendship above and beyond the mentoring relationship may develop.

4. *Performing.* You share a sense of loyalty and satisfaction with your mentor. You know and respect each other's style and work well together. The benefits of having developed a solid working relationship are paying off; you are "learning to teach better."

EARN AND KEEP YOUR MENTOR'S TRUST

Trust is vital to a mentoring relationship because it allows both you and your mentor to discuss situations beyond a superficial level and to work together in an atmosphere of mutual respect. Here are a couple of ways that you can contribute to the development and maintenance of trust between you and your mentor:

- *Respect confidentiality.* There may be times when your mentor decides to share something with you in confidence in order to help you better understand the crux of a situation. It may be that what is shared will expose a colleague's insecurity or lack of knowledge, thus leaving him or her vulnerable to ridicule if you repeat what was confided in you. Suppose, for example, that you ask your mentor whether you should observe Mr. Jones's class, and your mentor replies: "I recommend that you don't. Every time I pass his classroom, his students are out of control and he just ignores their behavior. I suspect he is burnt out." If you were to repeat your mentor's comments to a colleague, imagine what effect such a breach in confidentiality would have on your mentor-protégé relationship!

- *Walk the talk: That is, do what you said you would do.* A teacher-mentor I recently heard from—let's call her Phyllis—participated in a series of four workshops on brain-based learning. With her principal's approval, Phyllis asked her protégé, Brenda (not her real name), to participate in the series with her so that they could learn and discuss the strategy together. "I certainly will," was Brenda's reply to the invitation. "Thanks for asking me. I'll see you there." Brenda never showed up—not for the first session or for any others. In fact, she waited until the next day to apologize and promise to be there next time. Unfortunately, both Phyllis and Brenda avoided discussing the situation. Their mentoring relationship suffered accordingly.

Can you think of some other ways to develop and maintain trust between a protégé and mentor? Think about someone you trust. What does that person do or not do that makes it easy for you to trust her or him?

_____

_____

_____

CLARIFY COMMUNICATION

When two people converse, the receiver of the message will respond to what he or she perceives was said—not necessarily what the sender might have intended. If what the speaker intends to say and what the listener actually hears are the same, communication will be clear and unambiguous. If there is dissonance between the speaker's intent and the listener's perception, however, there will be not only misunderstanding but also potential damage to the relationship. Here are a few ways that you can help clarify communication between you and your mentor.

> *When two people converse, the receiver of the message will respond to what he or she perceives was said—not necessarily what the sender might have intended.*

Check Out Your Perceptions

Periodically check out the accuracy of your perception of what your mentor says to you. One way to do this is to restate in your own words what you heard and then allow your mentor to correct, clarify, or validate your restatement. For example:

Mentor: Your students were really focused today.

Protégé: Oh, you mean that today was an exception—that my students aren't usually focused?

Mentor: On the contrary. Your students are usually engaged. I consider what you did today, however, to have been exceptionally good. For example, remember when . . .

Respond to your mentor's statements and questions to his or her satisfaction before going on to another topic. This lets your mentor know that you listen to and respect what he or she says. Knowing this, your mentor will be more likely to share relevant information with you more often.

Share Feelings About Teaching

A powerful way to build and maintain a productive mentoring relationship is to share feelings about teaching. Feelings add depth to communication. It is important that you communicate and listen not just to words but also to feelings. For example, suppose Julie confides to her mentor that she is having trouble developing lesson plans, especially one for next week's third-period class. Her mentor replies, "I can see you are concerned about how to plan effective lessons. We can work on lesson planning next time we meet if you would like. Meanwhile, I will be happy to let you use my lesson plan for your class next week. It worked well for me, and hopefully it will for you, too." Julie says, "Wow, thanks! I'm glad that you feel comfortable sharing it with me. It must be a good one."

Recognizing the feelings associated with a statement shows that you are hearing your mentor at a deeper level than just the content of his or her words. Not only is attention to feelings helpful to the development of a good relationship, it also can open the way for the expression of concerns that may not be expressed and dealt with otherwise.

Attention to feelings can open the way for the expression of concerns that may not be expressed and dealt with otherwise.

Pay Attention to Body Language

Pay attention to and honor body language. Suppose that during a meeting with your mentor, she smiles and says to you, "Tell me how your class went this morning. I am really interested." Before you can answer, the smile disappears; your mentor glances at the clock and then starts fidgeting in her chair. Which message would you trust, the body language or the spoken word?

In all fairness, you may want to check out how accurately you perceived your mentor's nonverbal expressions by stating them. Doing so will give your mentor the opportunity to verify or correct your speculation.

To what extent do you need to be aware of the reactions that your use of body language evokes in others? For example, when you are listening to your mentor, would nodding your head occasionally cause him or her to feel that you were really paying attention? This really need not be a concern at all. If your intent and words are honest, your body language will follow suit.

Share Experiences

Where personalities and schedules permit, attend workshops and meetings with your mentor. Engage in informal conversation about teaching, politics, sports, or books—perhaps over coffee or lunch, even while jogging or playing golf. Using e-mail to keep in touch is also effective. All too often, mentors and protégés tend to limit their interactions to the routine, whereas expanding the range of the relationship can add to its depth and therefore its effectiveness.

> *All too often, mentors and protégés tend to limit their interactions to the routine, whereas expanding the range of the relationship can add to its depth and therefore its effectiveness.*

Show Respect

At times, in discussions of attributes of trust and relationships, the word *respect* surfaces. Most of the synonyms for *respect* in my dictionary do not define the word in the way I conceive of its application to the mentoring relationship. The dictionary's definition contains such words as *obeisance, homage, reverence, deference, esteem, honor, tribute,* and *adoration.*

During a recent conversation about the dynamics of the mentor-protégé relationship, Jenny, a colleague of mine, observed,

> It is natural that some people new to the profession lack confidence. My guess is that protégés who don't move beyond defensive responses to new situations miss out because they never make it past finding fault into genuinely understanding and honoring differences. These are the ones who lack respect for their mentors and the mentoring experience and are most likely to leave education early.

Like Jenny, when I use the word *respect* in the context of the mentor-protégé relationship, I mean the willingness to understand and honor differences. Although a young student teacher or beginning teacher, for example, may feel uncomfortable developing a mentoring relationship with an older person or one of a different gender or ethnicity, making the effort to understand and honor the differences is vital to the success of the relationship.

In addition to the age, ethnicity, gender, and experiences of others, differences requiring respect include the tradition, culture, and dynamics of the teaching-learning environment. For example, teachers placed in an urban school where the dynamics are very different from those of the middle-class environment that they may be most familiar with have difficulty respecting (i.e., understanding and honoring) its culture.

Phu N. Ly, a second-year teacher, advises new teachers to stay cool under fire. "Sometimes it is so easy to want to defend yourself with the principal or parents. I learned how to listen, to try to understand where they're coming from. Parents' concerns are very real" (DePaul, 1998, p. 9).

The bottom line is that although respect may not come easy, it is a vital ingredient in a relationship and is worth the time and effort to develop.

PRINCIPLES FOR SUCCESS

Protégés get the most out of being mentored when they are able to contribute to the development and maintenance of the mentoring partnership. You will be contributing to the mentoring relationship when you do the following:

- Do what you say you will do.
- Let your mentor know if you are unable to follow through on a promise, and suggest an alternative.
- Unless given permission by your mentor, treat in confidence whatever of a personal nature he or she tells you or what you observe.
- When your mentor offers some information or opinion or asks a question, respond to his or her statement or query before going on to another topic.
- Where you feel comfortable doing so, express your feelings as well as thoughts about a topic under discussion.
- Acknowledge, understand, and honor your mentor's feelings and ideas, even though you may not always agree with them.
- Periodically check out your assumptions of what your mentor was thinking and feeling as well as what was said.

CHAPTER TWO

Take Responsibility

What you may not understand is that for everything you have accomplished so far, there is way more out there that you haven't even seen yet. And it's not just going to come to you. You have to go get it yourselves.

Andrew Asensio, Salutatory Address,
Newington (Connecticut) High School
Graduation, June 2001

In the context of the mentoring process, your primary responsibility as a new teacher is "to learn to teach better." Put another way, your job as a new teacher is to develop the capacity and confidence to make your own informed decisions, enrich your own knowledge, and sharpen your own abilities regarding teaching and learning. The role of your mentor is to bring you, his or her protégé, to this level of professionalism. Sometimes, a mentor, for a variety of reasons, does not or cannot fulfill that role.

> *Your job as a new teacher is to develop the capacity and confidence to make your own informed decisions, enrich your own knowledge, and sharpen your own abilities regarding teaching and learning.*

Michelle J. faced such a situation. "Though my mentor was great and friendly," Michelle told me at the end of her first year of teaching, "I did not feel that I had the ongoing support I would have liked. It would have been wonderful for her to suggest a meeting time on a weekly basis, especially at the beginning of the school year, just to check in and review how my classes had gone that week. Sure, she said that although she didn't have a lot of time to spend with me, she would try to make time available if I had any questions. The problem was I had questions ALL THE TIME and would have liked her to initiate some feedback sessions."

DON'T WAIT, INSTIGATE

Michelle was fortunate in that she had a "great and friendly" mentor, but unfortunately the mentor did not meet her need for regular feedback sessions. Although Michelle would have liked her mentor to initiate a schedule of feedback sessions, she did not; in fact, her mentor probably did not even realize that Michelle wanted her to take that step. Michelle neglected to assume any responsibility for getting her need met; consequently, it was not.

How could Michelle have been proactive in this situation? Remember, she was invited by her mentor to ask for help if she had any questions. She could have introduced her request for a schedule of feedback sessions by thanking her mentor for that offer and then stating her need. She would have been well advised to have had a few alternative dates and times ready to discuss along with some suggestions about process and content. One way Michelle might have respected her mentor's limited availability of time would have been to suggest a trial period of 2 or 3 weeks before deciding on the length and frequency of future sessions. Can you think of anything else Michelle could have done or discussed with her mentor that might have helped address her need for regular feedback? Perhaps they could have used e-mail, for example, or exchanged journal entries. Write your thoughts below.

_____

_____

_____

FEEDBACK AND HOW TO RECEIVE IT

In the above scenario, Michelle wanted opportunity for feedback from her mentor. Just what is feedback, what is your responsibility in the process, and how can it help you learn to teach better?

Feedback is a way of providing people with information about their behavior and how those behaviors affect others. As in a guided missile system, feedback helps individuals keep their behavior "on target," and thus they are better able to achieve their goals. To be effective in working with others, we need to become skilled at giving, soliciting, and accepting feedback. (Luckner & Nadler, 1997, p. 88)

> *Feedback is a way of providing people with information about their behavior and how those behaviors affect others.*

Your mentor's responsibility is to provide you with feedback that is descriptive rather than evaluative, specific rather than general, solicited rather than imposed, and timely: that is, given as soon after the event as possible. To receive feedback when you want it, you need to request it; that is your responsibility. To benefit from feedback, you need to be open to hearing it; that, too, is your responsibility.

The following suggestions will help you be ready and able to receive feedback (Portner, 1998, p. 54):

- Focus on what is being said rather than how it is said.
- Focus on feedback as information rather than as criticism.
- Concentrate on receiving the new information rather than focusing on defending the old.
- Probe for specifics rather than accepting generalities.
- Focus on clarifying what has been said by summarizing the main points to the satisfaction of all parties.

WHEN TO GIVE FEEDBACK

Lonna S. is a mentor who not only specifically tells her protégés that they are in charge of their own learning but also has a rule that encourages them to be responsible. The rule:

if I say anything that you do not understand, it is my fault because it is my responsibility to mentor, and that includes explaining concepts, suggesting procedures, etc., so that you will understand. However, I won't know that you don't understand unless you tell me. So you must be responsible for your own learning by giving me feedback—by letting me know I didn't meet my responsibility for mentoring.

Consider this scenario. Earlier in the day, Betty and her mentor, Frank, had met for a postobservation conference, during which Frank pointed out Betty's difficulty in keeping a particular student engaged in the lesson and then went on to another subject. When Betty met Frank later in the day, during lunch, Frank asked her how she thought the conference went.

"Fine," Betty said, "except that when you pointed out that I did not engage Jimmy in the lesson and then you left the subject hanging with no opportunity for further discussion, I felt confused and unsure of what to do next."

Betty's feedback was descriptive, specific, solicited, and timely. As a result, Frank and Betty were able to pursue the problem of engaging students and identifying strategies to use in the future. From then on, Frank was also careful not to leave a subject during a conference with Betty until there was some degree of understanding and closure.

Can you think of other mentoring situations where feedback to the mentor by the protégé would be appropriate?

_____

_____

_____

MISMATCHED MENTORING RELATIONSHIPS

Melanie P. was a business education major at a large southern university. She was assigned to work with a cooperating teacher with whom she could not get along. When asked to share her experiences during her student-teaching internship, Melanie had a lot to say about how that mentoring relationship was a negative experience. But now, seeing through the 20/20 lens of hindsight, Melanie understands that she had the ability to have taken responsibility for changing the situation. Her advice to potential interns and protégés is "Explore your choices closely. If you are assigned a mentor-teacher that you feel you cannot work with, examine alternatives." I would add to Melanie's advice that prior to formally requesting a change of mentors, consider taking responsibility for trying to improve the relationship by working to get the most you can from the existing situation.

Along somewhat the same lines, Julie, an education major at another university, told me that, as part of her prepracticum, she was given a 6-week assignment to observe a particular teacher in one of the city's elementary schools. After spending 3 days in the teacher's classroom, Julie became very upset with her assignment. It seems the teacher she was observing was a first-year teacher, was not able to control her class very well, had no lesson plans, and used poor grammar. The professor refused Julie's request to change to another teacher in the same school, one whom she respected and who happened to be mentor to the first-year teacher Julie was observing. Julie asked me to suggest ways she might get the most out of her observations and also how to go about getting help from the mentor-teacher she respected. Here is a summary of my response:

Your overall goal, Julie, is to analyze and learn from both the positive and negative happenings in the classroom. This will be easier to do if you focus your observations on one area at a time—for example,

> *Your overall goal is to analyze and learn from both the positive and negative happenings in the classroom.*

classroom management. Of course, you will need to know what to look for, how to reflect on what you observe, and what other strategies might be used in similar situations. Here is where your respected teacher-mentor can help. If that person is willing, *and* the teacher you are observing agrees, ask her (a) What goes into effective classroom management and how do I recognize it? and (b) Would you please sit in on a portion of a class with me and help me reflect on what I observed?

RESPONSIBILITY TO YOURSELF

It is difficult to establish a healthy, safe, and nurturing classroom environment if you yourself are not well centered. Christopher

Markofski, a first-year kindergarten teacher in Washington, insists that

> teachers can't forget about the importance of their own mental, [emotional,] and physical health or they will fall apart. Find time to go out with your colleagues to talk about mutual ideas and problems—let off steam. There are tons of kids sneezing and coughing on you every day. You need to be healthy to be a good teacher. I jog in the morning like any good prizefighter. (DePaul, 1998, p. 13)

RESPONSIBILITY TO OTHERS

If you are a newly trained teacher recently exposed to the application of new technologies and research to education, and if you are a partner in a mentor/protégé relationship, you have a responsibility to help others meet their needs in addition to meeting your own. Judith S., a mentor-teacher, puts it this way: "I expect and encourage my protégés to contribute to the school's library of new ideas at the same time that they are drawing from experienced teachers." She goes on to ask, "Shouldn't new teachers be coming to the table with new technological skills and fresh techniques to share with the old guard so that we can grow from their youth?"

New teachers can also help the mentoring program in general by participating in the program's evaluation and revision efforts. Chapter 9, "Give Back," discusses some other ways a novice can contribute to his or her school's development and culture.

GET TO KNOW YOUR PRINCIPAL

Amy DePaul (2000) suggests that beginning teachers can take responsibility for building a professional relationship with their principals by

- Asking for professional development opportunities
- Seeking assistance in setting up a mentor relationship if a program is not already in place
- Requesting that the principal visit their classroom and give constructive feedback prior to the formal evaluation period (p. 18)

CLARIFY GROUND RULES EARLY

Early in your relationship with a mentor, discuss expectations and what you would like to get out of the mentoring experience. Agree on objectives for the relationship. Sort out roles and boundaries. Set schedules. Present your positions and feelings honestly so that there will be no false assumptions.

For example, here is a conversation between a mentor and a protégé:

Mentor: Since time for us to meet during school hours is at a premium, let's meet in the teachers' room at 7:00 every Monday morning [a half hour before teachers are required to arrive] to touch bases and plan for the week.

Protégé: I know we can use the time, but I'm in a carpool. We don't get here until about 7:30. How about after school? I have to wait for the driver then anyhow.

Mentor: Not so good for me. I usually use that time to correct papers or review plans for the next day. Is there any way you can get here early on Mondays?

Protégé: I don't know. . . . Well, okay. I'll be willing to drive my own car on Mondays if you really think it's the best time.

Mentor: I'll tell you what. Let's meet in the morning this coming Monday—coffee's on me—and after school next time. If it works out, we can alternate this way. How does that sound?

Protégé: It's a deal. See you at 7:00 Monday morning.

PRINCIPLES FOR SUCCESS

Protégés get the most out of being mentored when they are able to take responsibility and be proactive in the mentoring process. You will be taking responsibility when you do the following:

- ◆ Take the initiative when it comes to having your needs as a protégé met.
- ◆ Avoid making assumptions about your mentor's plans and expectations.
- ◆ Solicit feedback from your mentor as a way to improve your teaching.
- ◆ Receive feedback objectively.
- ◆ Attempt to construct ways to learn from seemingly untenable situations.
- ◆ Take responsibility for your personal well-being.
- ◆ Contribute to the learning of other educators.

CHAPTER THREE

Observe

Who knows the flower best—the one who reads about it in a book, or the one who finds it wild on the mountainside?

Alexander David-Neel

It is common practice for a mentor to observe a protégé in the classroom. It is less common that a mentor will invite a protégé to observe him or her in action. There is much that can be learned from both scenarios. The protégé who takes responsibility for his or her own learning will do whatever he or she can to see to it that both types of observations take place. In this chapter, we will discuss the protégé's observation of others.

BE AN OBJECTIVE OBSERVER

While in another's classroom, strive to be an objective observer—a human video camera—recording what is going on. Resist the temptation to become a participant. It is difficult to participate and observe objectively at the same time. Also,

> *While in another's classroom, strive to be an objective observer. Resist the temptation to become a participant.*

understand that your unfamiliar presence in the classroom, however unobtrusive, will have some influence on what is being observed. When you observe someone else's class, you are actually observing a class being observed.

WHAT TO OBSERVE

When you first watch someone else teach, you may want simply to get an overall feel for that person's style and teaching strategies. Soon, however, you will want to focus on that person's particular teaching behaviors. It will be especially valuable if you can meet with the person whom you observe before the class to discuss what to expect and again, shortly after the class, to discuss what you observed. For example, after observing a class, a student teacher asked, "I noticed that students quieted down when you put a finger to the side of your nose. What was that all about?"

When you are observing a classroom, it will help if you focus on only one aspect at a time.

Once you are comfortable as an observer and have a general sense of the classroom you are observing, it will help if you focus on only one aspect at a time. Juan R. (not his real name), a first-year teacher in a big-city elementary school, swears that he learned more by spending 30 minutes in his mentor's class focusing on the way she interacted with students than from any education course. As he put it, "It was a revelation to watch her keep order without relying on the gimmicks that were drilled into us in training programs, as if children were nematodes in a Skinnerian laboratory."

Here are some observable teaching behaviors on which you can focus:

- How does the teacher establish and maintain a positive social and emotional atmosphere in the learning environment? For example, the teacher demonstrates patience and acceptance of students through positive verbal and nonverbal exchanges.
- How does the teacher create a climate that encourages all students to achieve? For example, the teacher exhibits expectations for success by communicating expectations through approaches to assigning tasks, rewarding student effort, and providing help and encouragement.
- To the extent it is under her or his control, how does the teacher establish a physical environment that is safe and conducive to learning? For example, the teacher has

arranged chairs, desks, and tables in such a way as to allow for group interaction while at the same time providing for rapid and safe movement in and out of the physical space formed by that arrangement.

- How does the teacher communicate and reinforce appropriate standards of behavior for the students? For example, the teacher has established, administered, and maintained rules for student behavior.

- How does the teacher vary methodologies in relation to diversity in the classroom? For example, the teacher provides accommodations for students with special needs; addresses the individual learning styles of students; and avoids sarcasm, disparaging remarks, sexist and racial comments, and scapegoating.

- How does the teacher initiate a lesson? For example, the teacher previews with students what is to be learned, why it is to be learned, and how it relates to past or future learning.

What other teaching behaviors might you want to observe?

_____

_____

_____

EXPAND YOUR VIEW

The opportunity to learn by watching others can extend beyond observing your "official" mentor. Lisa R., who is fulfilling her teaching internship requirement as a graduate student at the University

The opportunity to learn by watching others can extend beyond observing your "official" mentor.

of Tennessee, suggests to other interns, "Watch your mentoring teacher teach as much as possible. Then, to get a broader view, go watch at least two other teachers teaching the same subject you want to teach."

Cathy Foltz is a new teacher in a small school district. Although she has an assigned mentor, she has also found many of the other experienced teachers to be, as she puts it, "extremely generous about helping 'the new guy.'" I asked Cathy what advice she had for a new teacher or intern. "My best advice," she said, "would be to be open to the mentor's suggestions, but don't lock yourself into following one person. Talk with and observe other experienced teachers."

As you plan to observe teachers in your school or in another, you should be sure that the principal of that school not only is aware of your plans but also has agreed to your arrangements.

DON'T IMITATE, CREATE

Several years ago, David S. (not his real name) applied to a human resource company as a time management trainer. David had conducted time management classes before, with considerable success, and had even developed his own materials. All this, coupled with the fact that he was an experienced and respected public school teacher, led both David and the human resource company to believe that he would be ideal for the job. They hired him and assigned Sam C. (also, not his real name) as David's mentor. David began by observing his mentor, Sam, conduct a training session so that, as Sam told him, "he could see the right way to do it." Then David was given a script to memorize and follow while he was conducting the training. Finally, Sam observed his protégé present his first "for real" training session.

It was a disaster! David was supposed to follow the script but could not. It clashed with his personal teaching style, and, as he told me, "the company's rules required me to stay on track and ignore teachable moments—you know, those questions and reactions that cry out for something more." David admitted he became so flustered that Sam had to take over. Needless to say, that was the end of David's job with that company. "In all fairness, though," David told me later, "the company did let me use many of my own materials, and they did have employees—like Sam—who successfully used their methods. On the positive side," he went on, "I did learn a few things from observing Sam—especially how to use technology to make presentations. I also realized that effective teaching can take many forms."

Unlike Sam's company, public schools may not require teachers to teach to a script when it comes to instructional strategies and methods (i.e., *how* to teach). As David observed, effective teaching can take many forms. Curriculum, however (i.e., *what* to teach), is usually prescribed and often follows a specific framework.

> By all means, you should learn and study from successes in your field. There is no need to reinvent the wheel, and you shorten your learning curve by [observing] what others have done. . . . But remember to take what you learn and *adapt* it to suit your particular abilities. (Keller, 2001, p. 3)

PRINCIPLES FOR SUCCESS

Protégés get the most out of being mentored when they not only take advantage of invitations to observe others teach but also create their own opportunities. When you observe others, you will benefit most when you do the following:

- Identify teachers other than your mentor whom you would like to observe.
- Try to arrange opportunities to observe others when invitations to do so are not forthcoming.
- Inform the principal of any observation visits you plan to carry out.
- Withhold judgment until you have had the opportunity to reflect on and consider what you have observed.
- Focus on a particular aspect of the class or lesson you are observing.

CHAPTER FOUR

Ask

If you wanted to know what it's like to walk on the moon, you'd interview an astronaut. If you wanted insights on playing Hamlet, you'd study the performance of a Shakespearean actor. And if you wanted to know what the first year of teaching school is like, well . . .

Sharon A. Bobbitt

WHOM TO ASK

Mentors aren't the only source of help for new teachers. Teachers who just completed their first year can also have a lot of suggestions to offer new teachers who follow them—if they are asked. Amy DePaul (1998) asked first-year teachers for any advice they would like to pass along. Among the many tips and strategies she received, one from Phu N. Ly, a second-grade teacher, is especially pertinent to this discussion. Ly said, "Learn how to listen." You may not have the opportunity to listen to answers to things you want to know unless you ask.

In addition to your mentor and second-year teachers, there are others you can ask for help. Older, more experienced teachers love to be asked for their opinion and advice too. "If you feel over-whelmed by paperwork," suggests Sharon, a second-year teacher, "ask experienced colleagues how they

Older, more experienced teachers love to be asked for their opinion and advice.

manage it. Even if you feel your classroom is going well, ask them how they do their bulletin boards, how often they do read-aloud—whatever. If you get a few good ideas from them—and chances are you will—it doesn't hurt to tell them so and to thank them."

WHERE TO ASK

In addition to face-to-face conversations, there are other ways beginners have found to ask older colleagues for help. A first-year teacher in a suburban district in New England let it be known during a faculty meeting that she would very much appreciate ideas and materials from her experienced colleagues. Not only has she personally received some useful worksheets and ideas for projects, but also the idea of sharing has spread throughout the school so that now, as a result of her request, if a teacher tries something new in class and it works, it is automatically shared with the entire faculty.

Another new sixth-grade teacher put up a "want ad" in the teachers' room. She advertised for weather information for a unit on agriculture. A fifth-grade teacher answered the ad.

HOW TO ASK

When you ask for help, ask assertively. To be assertive is to honor your own basic rights without violating the basic human rights of others (Jakubowski-Spector, 1973). As a protégé, you have the right to be assertive when you ask for help, just as the person you ask has the right to refuse. For example, you have the right to ask your mentor for permission to use a new lesson plan he or she developed, and your mentor can respond just as assertively by saying, "I appreciate your interest in the lesson plan, but it has not yet been tested, so I prefer not to share it yet."

Being assertive does not mean being aggressive—that is, invading the other person's boundaries. For example, a request like "Hey, give me your lesson plan to use" or a response like "Certainly not!" or "Don't be stupid" is aggressive because it violates the other person's right to courtesy and respect. On the other hand, being assertive does not mean allowing one's own boundaries to be restricted. For example, the mentor's nonassertive response to the request to see a lesson plan would have been to share the lesson plan even though he or she did not really want to.

You may not get what you ask for unless you yourself are clear about what it is you want.

Even if you are assertive, you may not get what you ask for unless you yourself are clear about what it is you want.

WHAT TO ASK FOR

What are you really asking for when you make a request for help? Understanding what type of request you are making can help you phrase your question to best elicit the kind of response you want.

Understanding what type of request you are making can help you phrase your question to best elicit the kind of response you want.

Gazda, Asbury, Balzer, Childers, and Walters (1991) developed a framework that identifies several types of requests for help.

One type of request is a request for action. Do you want the person to do something? If so, say so. For example, suppose you want your mentor to look at and comment on your new lesson plan, and you say, "I have developed a lesson plan, but I'm not sure how good it is." He or she may or may not offer to look at it, and you may not get the type of response you really want. On the other hand, "Please critique my new lesson plan" directly asks for the desired response—in this case, action.

Another type of request is for information: for example, "Where is the copy machine located?" rather than "Can I get this copied?"

A third type of request is for understanding or emotional support. This is more difficult to ask for than the other types, and you may find yourself making such a request with an expression of anger or frustration or with nonverbal cues such as a sigh. For example, saying to a mentor, "I'm going to have my first meeting with a parent tomorrow. What should I say?" may seem to be a request for information, but you may also be signaling for emotional support. It can be difficult, but if you really want and need your mentor's understanding, you might express your feelings by saying, for example, "Will the parents think I'm too young to be a teacher?" or "What if I make a fool of myself?"

Jennifer, a first-year teacher, needed to ask for emotional support. She worked in a school district that had, as she put it, "a very flexible curriculum that caused me a great deal of frustration. Though I loved the freedom and flexibility to be creative," she explained, "I felt I did not always know if I was doing the right things to best help my students. I felt very lonely and isolated, and I just didn't know if I was really cut out for teaching." Jennifer added that she felt uncomfortable asking Gwen, her mentor, for emotional support. She could not bring herself to talk to her principal or other teachers in her district about her feelings either, so she looked elsewhere for emotional support—the Internet. It paid off. Jennifer received what she was looking for from supportive teachers on-line.

Now, if you were to ask a group of beginning teachers what specific kind of help they needed from a mentor, many would tell you—as they consistently tell me and other researchers—that they needed help with discipline, classroom management, and lesson planning. In addition, most would indicate that they needed information about school policies and procedures, appreciated timely feedback, and hungered for friendly support (Portner, 1998). Dan L., a longtime mentor in a large school district, notes that questions from new teachers range from the basics—finding restrooms and making photocopies—to more complicated issues, such as the school culture and parent involvement.

When Betty S. got her first teaching job, she felt well prepared. Several weeks prior to the start of school, she read everything she could get her hands on about classroom management and mathematics, her subject. She got copies of the textbook she would use and downloaded state objectives from the Internet. At the end of her first year of teaching, she had the following to say about the time she spent preparing. On Teacher Net's Beginning Teacher Chatboard, Betty wrote,

> In hindsight, I also wish that I'd called the principal and gotten the names of a couple of teachers from the math department who would be willing to meet with me or talk to me over the

phone to answer questions. And then I'd have picked their brains on how they did things, what the student[s] at the school were like, how supportive the administration was, what kinds of problems they have with students/parents/ administration, how they set up grading, how often did they test, how many assemblies could I expect, when will I know how many students are in each class, where do I get supplies, and who's friendly in the office. The list can go on and on. (7/14/01)

Jamie, a fifth-grade teacher also posting on Teacher Net's Beginning Teacher Chatboard, lets new teachers know that although experienced teachers can be very supportive, they might have forgotten all the little things that new teachers might need. "For example, veteran teachers may not remember how much new teachers and student teachers love to collect worksheets, lesson plans, and other such resources" (7/15/01).

Amy DePaul (2000) quotes a first-year teacher who wrote, "I realized that it was time to ask [veteran teachers] questions, put my time and energy to better use for my students and myself. Today, I wouldn't dream of beginning a new unit without inquiring about resources and possible models" (p. 8).

What specific materials would you like to ask your experienced colleagues to set aside for you? List them below.

_____

_____

_____

WHY ASK?

Joan (not her real name) is a student teacher. It was during the second week of her practicum/internship in a vocational high school that she was first exposed to the concept of writing across the curriculum. Joan was observing her cooperating teacher, Ms. Perry (not her real name), teach a ninth-grade English class. "You've probably seen this format in some of your other academic classes," Ms. Perry said to her students. "We will be using this format for our writing here as well. In the upper left-hand corner will be the FCAs, or Focus Correction Areas. There will be one, two, or three areas for you to focus on in your assigned piece of writing."

Focus Correction Areas?[1] Joan hadn't heard the term before. She was curious. If the students knew about it—and she was going to be teaching them soon—she had better know about it too.

Later that day, during their prep period, Joan asked Ms. Perry, "What are Focus Correction Areas? You used the term with the ninth graders this morning."

"FCAs?" Ms. Perry answered. "Why, they're an element of *Writing Across the Curriculum*. They're part of a writing program we use in all the academic classes."

Joan asked Ms. Perry and the other teachers, "Do any of you have materials about FCAs and *Writing Across the Curriculum?*"

They promised to look, but neither Ms. Perry nor the other teachers were able to find more than a couple of worksheets, although they all remembered having received more materials. Joan wanted her own complete set of materials. She asked Ms. Perry where she could get some.

"The office should have some on file," Ms. Perry suggested.

Joan asked the office secretary, but she could not locate any.

Joan asked the secretary, "Who else may be able to help me?"

"The principal," she answered, "but she's not in just now."

"Can I leave a note in her mailbox?"

"She'll get it quicker if you tape it to her office door."

The next day, Joan received a complete set of materials. She told me that shortly after receiving the materials, a student asked for her help with an assignment involving FCAs. She was delighted to have been able to respond to the student's request. Joan might have ignored Ms. Perry's reference to FCAs or waited until she actually took over a class and had to plan a lesson, but she decided to be proactive—to ask.

Who did she ask? Her cooperating teacher, other teachers, the secretary, and the principal.

Where did she ask? She asked where she supposed the answer would be most readily available, in the teachers' room, and then in the school office.

How did she ask? Assertively through the use of direct questions, and, at the suggestion of the secretary, with a note taped to a door.

What did she ask for? She asked for what she would need in the not-too-distant future. She asked for information ("What are

FCAs? What is *Writing Across the Curriculum?*") and action ("Please provide me with materials.").

Why did she ask? Because she felt a need to know, to have, and to learn.

NOTE

1. Focus Correction Areas are a set of criteria for assigning and evaluating student writing developed by John Collins (1992).

PRINCIPLES FOR SUCCESS

Protégés get the most out of being mentored when they are able to ask for help; especially when they know who and how to ask. You will get helpful responses to your requests when you do the following:

- Understand that you have not only the responsibility but also the right to ask your mentor for help.
- Be comfortable about asking other teachers for help.
- Ask for help in ways other than verbally.
- Be willing to ask teachers outside your school and district for help.
- Respect your right to ask for help as long as you do not infringe on the rights of others by doing so.
- Respect the right of others to deny your request.
- When you ask for help, decide whether you are asking for action, information, or emotional support.
- Limit your questions and requests to what you really want or need.

CHAPTER FIVE

Chart Your Course

It is not enough to just do your best or work hard. You must know what to work on.

Edward Deming

Last spring, the National Football League's New England Patriots welcomed 10 rookie free agents and 10 draft choices to a minicamp. "The biggest problem with the rookies right now," lamented coach Bill Belichick, "is that they don't know what they don't know."

FIND OUT WHAT YOU DON'T KNOW

"I feel so disorganized. I don't know if I will make it through my first year." This was the cry for help that Jennifer sent out to other teachers on an Internet chatboard.

Emma had taught for 3 years. Here was the gist of her reply to Jennifer. "Don't give up!" she urged. "Many new teachers have these feelings. You are still learning and not yet on top of things. It doesn't mean you aren't doing a good job, you just haven't had enough experience yet to know what works and what doesn't."

If you are serious about learning to teach better, you will need to know what you don't know before you can decide what you need to learn. As Confucius observed, "To know what you

If you are serious about learning to teach better, you will need to know what you don't know before you can decide what you need to learn.

know and know what you don't know is the characteristic of one who knows."

One way to start finding out what you know and don't know is to reflect on how well you are able to deal with specific areas you are facing now. You need to ask yourself and answer honestly the question "Do I have the knowledge to face this situation with confidence?"

If you are not teaching yet and expect to be soon, you can ask experienced teachers to tell you what situations you might face when you start teaching. You can then ask yourself, "Will I have the knowledge to face these kinds of situations with confidence if and when they occur?"

To get you started, the Assessment of Knowledge and Confidence (see the form on page 35) contains a list of 20 areas that typically contribute to the angst of being a new teacher. I have left room for you (and your mentor) to add others. In the blank in front of each list item, give a rating that indicates your estimate of the extent of your knowledge and confidence regarding the situation, using a scale of 1 to 4 as follows:

1 = I have very little knowledge of this.

2 = I have some knowledge, but I'm not sure I can apply it.

3 = I have enough knowledge and comfort level to get by.

4 = I have a solid knowledge base and high level of confidence.

Next, in the blank following each list item, have your mentor give a rating that indicates his or her assessment of you using the scale below:

1 = You have very little knowledge of this.

2 = You have some knowledge, but I'm not sure you can apply it.

3 = You have enough knowledge and comfort level to get by.

4 = You have a solid knowledge base and high level of confidence.

ASSESSMENT OF
KNOWLEDGE AND CONFIDENCE

Your Rating		*Mentor's Rating*
____	State standards and frameworks	____
____	Cultural diversity	____
____	Parent conferences	____
____	Working with ESL (English as a Second Language) students	____
____	Consequencing or disciplining students	____
____	Classroom management	____
____	Creating a safe learning environment	____
____	Working with special-needs students	____
____	Student learning styles and how to adapt curriculum to accommodate	____
____	Assessing and grading students	____
____	Developing lesson plans	____
____	Finding and using curricular and professional resources	____
____	Using technology in the classroom	____
____	Requesting supplies and equipment	____
____	Teacher evaluation procedures	____
____	Personal organization (e.g., time and stress management, record keeping)	____
____	Using a variety of instructional strategies	____
____	Using school phone, copier, fax, etc.	____
____	Teacher contract particulars	____
____	Dealing with emergencies	____

Other Categories:

____	_____	____
____	_____	____
____	_____	____
____	_____	____

Discuss the two sets of ratings with your mentor. Probe more deeply into any item where your own ratings differ from your mentor's by three or four points in order to clarify and learn from the reason for such a discrepancy.

Carr, Herman, and Harris (2001) have developed the Monthly Focus Chart, a comprehensive set of concerns that protégés may have as they go through their first year of teaching. The concerns are organized by month (August through April) and are grouped into the following categories: informational, instructional, personal, management, results, and collaboration. In August, for example, a protégé will want to become familiar with the physical setup of the school and location of key facilities, know how to acquire necessary supplies, and be acquainted with the school's student discipline policies. In January, major concerns include being familiar with resources available from state and federal programs, preparing students to take upcoming state exams, and preparing postholiday lesson plans.

The Center for Curriculum Renewal, developers of the Monthly Focus Chart, has agreed to provide the chart to readers of this book who call 802-860-6802 or who e-mail their request to <CCRlearn@aol.com>.

SET PRIORITIES

Trying to learn everything you need to know at the same time that you are dealing with all the other things new teachers have to do is totally unrealistic. So the next step is to set priorities—to determine what area(s) to tackle first. Obviously, the issues to which you and your mentor have assigned the lowest ratings will need the most attention, but the "urgency factor" also needs to be considered. In other words, the areas with the lowest ratings *and* in need of immediate attention are your top priorities and should be addressed first.

The areas in the Assessment of Knowledge and Confidence that have the lowest ratings and *are in need of immediate attention are your top priorities and should be addressed first.*

Write down your two highest priorities on the blanks provided on the next page. Once you have addressed one to your satisfaction, cross it off and add another in its place.

1. _____

2. _____

As part of the discussion of priorities with your mentor, it would prove enlightening to identify and clarify local priorities. Taking time to do this will help you to better understand the school's and district's culture and policies.

IDENTIFY RESOURCES

Next, identify some resources that can help you learn more about these top priorities. Your mentor and supervisor, of course, are major resources, but other teachers, secretaries, custodians, college faculty members, professional publications, local businesses, government agencies, professional organizations, regional and state education departments, electronic and printed materials (see Resource A), family, and friends are also potential resources. Harry Wong (2001) contends that "what a new teacher needs and deserves is a tutor, . . . a group of teachers, staff developers, and administrators who will *teach* that new teacher and get him or her up to speed quickly" (p. 47).

List your potential resources in the space below. Be specific as to names, and indicate how, where, and/or when you can best access them.

Resource	Notes
_____	_____
_____	_____
_____	_____
_____	_____
_____	_____
_____	_____

Will Rogers once said, "Even if you're on the right track, you'll get run over if you just sit there." So now that you are on the right track—that is, you are a rookie who knows what you don't know—you can begin to work on what you still need to learn in order to teach better. Cultivate the habit of including on your daily or weekly to-do list something having to do with addressing your priorities. If an activity will take several hours to complete and you don't have that large a block of time available on a given day, plan to spend only 10 or 15 minutes on that task. By the end of a week or two, you will have completed the activity. And by the way, don't forget to share your progress with your mentor.

Cultivate the habit of including on your daily or weekly to-do list something having to do with addressing your priorities.

THE POWER OF PLANNING

Your completed plan for improvement will focus on a specific goal, delineate resources, and perhaps set time lines. Hopefully, you will carry out your plan and it will help you "learn to teach better."

Robby Champion (2001) points out an additional benefit you will derive from your plan. "The finished action plan," she writes, "is so simple and straightforward that the power of the strategic thinking involved in developing it easily can be missed" (p. 62). In other words, the processes of discovering what you don't know, setting priorities, identifying resources, and deciding how and when to carry out your plan are, in and of themselves, dynamic learning experiences. You learn about your needs, your teaching environment, and your sources of support; you add value and substance to your understanding and philosophy of teaching; and you strengthen your feelings of order and control over your professional development.

The processes of discovering what you don't know, setting priorities, identifying resources, and deciding how and when to carry out your plan are, in and of themselves, dynamic learning experiences.

PRINCIPLES FOR SUCCESS

Protégés get the most out of being mentored when they are aware of what they still need to know and how and where to address those needs. You will be able to plan ahead and better address your needs when you can do the following:

- If you are not sure of something, seek more information.
- Identify and deal with the most pressing need-to-know items first.
- Seek out and use resources to help you address your priorities.
- Share your progress with your mentor.

CHAPTER SIX

Network

The best ideas are common property.

Lucius Annaeus Seneca

If your mentor, school, or district does not provide the opportunity to interact periodically with other new teachers, consider taking the initiative and creating the opportunity yourself.

Just about all educators, especially beginning ones, need inspiration and encouragement from others to continue to learn and grow professionally. If your mentor, school, or district does not provide the opportunity to interact periodically with other new teachers, consider taking the initiative and creating the opportunity yourself.

SUPPORT FROM COLLEGIAL GROUPS

Amy DePaul (1998) found that "new teachers who worked in teams . . . or had contact with other first year teachers, relished the camaraderie" (p. 14). She cited comments by several new teachers about ways to break the feeling of professional isolation. A seventh-grade teacher in New York, for example, suggested that in addition to having a mentor,

It would . . . be helpful to connect [first-year with second-year] teachers. The second-year teachers would have fresh memories of experiences that the first-year teachers would encounter and would be able to give them some forewarning and suggestions regarding how to best handle those experiences. (p. 15)

A sixth-grade teacher in Washington, D.C., provides another scenario:

All first-year teachers in my district meet three times a month. We write a journal every week with problems and successes. I am able to use other teachers' ideas for my own classes. . . . I never feel alone or stranded for ideas.

Student teachers too can benefit from meeting regularly with their colleagues. Some teacher-preparation programs provide an opportunity to do so; others do not. Jeannette W., a kindergarten teacher, wishes her college had aided students in establishing cohort groups. "The opportunity," she said, "would have provided me with avenues for in-depth discussion and for the brainstorming of ideas."

Ilene L. is an experienced mentor-teacher who leads a group of her district's first-year teachers in weekly get-togethers to discuss such aspects of their jobs as engaging and grading students, creating lesson plans, and parent-teacher conferencing. Ilene considers these sessions to be very important to the retention and growth of new teachers. "This job," she tells her charges, "will take everything you can give it. To try to do that all alone, without a support group, especially in the first year, you need the reassurance and support. You need human contact."

If you are a new or student teacher experiencing feelings of professional isolation, you may want to help organize a new teachers' support and discussion group in your school or college. Here are some guidelines.

If you are a new or student teacher experiencing feelings of professional isolation, you may want to help organize a new teachers' support and discussion group in your school or college.

GUIDELINES FOR SUPPORT AND DISCUSSION GROUPS

1. Makeup of the group

   - Membership should be limited to 3 to 10 beginning or student teachers facilitated by an experienced mentor-teacher.
   - Membership may be voluntary.

2. Meetings

   - Schedule meetings once a week or once every other week (avoid Fridays, holiday weeks, and weeks with major school events).
   - Limit meetings to 45 minutes to 1 hour in duration.
   - Meet before or after the school day.
   - Meetings can be held in other than school settings.
   - Set and distribute the agenda ahead of time.

3. Focus

   - The meeting should focus on teaching and learning.
   - Each meeting should be limited to one or two key issues.
   - It is okay to seek support for personal issues (allow time on agenda).
   - Team building and closure activities are encouraged.

4. Materials to support discussions

   - Current curricula and standards
   - School handbook
   - Professional development schedule
   - Personal journals and reflections
   - Commercial videos
   - Professional publications

5. Rules

   - Shared information is confidential.
   - Meetings are not gripe sessions.
   - Stick to the topic.
   - Decide whether new members are welcome to the group.
   - Establish and maintain expectations and routines.

NETWORKING ON THE INTERNET

The Internet offers an avenue for networking that is not limited by time or space. There is a wealth of chatrooms and chatboards on the Web where student teachers, new teachers, and experienced teachers can pose and answer questions, seek emotional support, and participate in professional discussions. Resource A in this book provides an annotated listing of such aids.

There is also at least one professional association (National Association for Beginning Teachers) devoted entirely to beginning teachers. Other professional associations, such as the Association of Supervision and Curriculum Development (ASCD) and the American Educational Research Association (AERA), have special interest groups (SIGs) for members who are in teacher preparation programs. Most education associations and organizations encourage new teachers to join and attend their conferences. These professional events provide excellent opportunities not only for learning but also for meeting, mutually supporting, and interacting professionally with other student teachers and new teachers from around the country and the world. Most education associations and organizations post their conference schedules on their Web pages. Resource B is a list of professional organizations and their Web pages.

WORKING WITH COLLEGE AND UNIVERSITY PROFESSORS AND COHORTS

Amy DePaul (2000) observes that "many teachers say they would benefit if teacher preparation programs monitored the progress of their graduates. . . . [They] could keep [us] informed of professional development opportunities or lectures so that new teachers could retain a connection to the latest research" (p. 19).

Although some state accreditation policies recommend that teacher education programs maintain some sort of connection with their graduates, some teachers tell me that professors, by and large, have not continued to keep them informed; they acknowledge that it is ultimately their responsibility to keep in touch with their professors, education programs, and classmates. For example, DePaul (2000) writes that "first year teacher Mara Esposito is still involved in her preparation program. . . . She and her classmates get together annually, and they have a newsletter about their experiences" (p. 19). Ms. Esposito also suggests that recent graduates should give their professors feedback on how their classes prepared them for a teaching career and that they should offer to visit the professors' classes and describe their professional experiences (p. 20).

Recent graduates should give their professors feedback on how their classes prepared them for a teaching career.

Do you know or can you think of other ways to network with peers for support and information? If so, list them below:

_____

_____

_____

I would appreciate a copy of your list so that I can share it with others. You can e-mail it to me at

Portner_Associates@ Compuserve.com.

PRINCIPLES FOR SUCCESS

Protégés get the most out of being mentored when, in addition to working with their mentors, they seek out and create opportunities to exchange information and support with their peers. You will have created opportunities to interact professionally with peers when you do the following:

- ♦ Join the peer support/learning group that your school district or college provides.
- ♦ Help organize a support and discussion group if no such opportunity for networking is provided by your school district or college.
- ♦ Subscribe to and use Internet chatboards for teachers (see Resources A and C).

CHAPTER SEVEN

Take Informed Risks

Almost everything a new teacher and student teacher does is a risk—it is all new territory.

Jennifer Seydel

As a student teacher, Kris learned very quickly that classroom management, not content, was his albatross. Because his cooperating teacher, Rosa, chose to be in the classroom whenever he taught, Kris found it difficult to learn how to discipline because Rosa always came to his rescue. One day, a particular discipline problem arose while he was teaching, and Kris risked privately asking his cooperating teacher to please leave the room. He wanted to try handling the problem by himself. Rosa left, and as Kris tells it, "That's when I really discovered what I knew and didn't know about classroom management."

Like Kris, you may decide to take a small risk—to make a small change—in order to learn to teach better. If you are going to boldly venture into new territory, however, then your decision to do so should be an informed one. Remember, change to the status quo is difficult for many to accept. *You may ask yourself, "Do I dare take risks?" The answer is a resounding Yes.* As a student teacher or new teacher, you are probably unfamiliar with much of the history and rationale behind the actions and procedures of your colleagues, department, school, and district. If you challenge those things, you run the risk of not only causing disruption but also losing the respect and support of your peers. Not only is it risky for "the new kid on the block" to challenge the culture, tradition, or modus operandi of an individual colleague, a school, or a school system, but it may also prove to be imprudent.

Given what I just cautioned against, you might well ask yourself, "Do I dare take risks?" The answer is a resounding *Yes*. As I stressed in the introduction of this book, the job of a new teacher—indeed, any teacher—is to learn to teach better. Learning implies change. Change implies risk.

> *Learning implies change.*
> *Change implies risk.*

You can learn to risk. That is to say, you can develop the skills and understanding (and hopefully the wisdom) to be an informed risk taker. Start small. Initially, any risks you take should be confined to areas like your own teaching style (try walking in front of the desk on occasion) or the use of materials (try overheads instead of the chalkboard).

Somewhere down the line, however, you may become aware of something outside your immediate control that you feel needs to be done differently.

LOOK BEFORE YOU LEAP

Before you rush headlong into doing something new or differently that involves others, take the time to examine the impulse through several lenses.

To begin with, look at the moral and ethical implications of taking the risk. In the medical profession, new doctors take the Hippocratic oath, which begins "First, do no harm." The same should apply for new teachers. While we all may make mistakes when learning, the right of a protégé to learn to be a better teacher does not include the right to threaten his or her own or someone else's physical or emotional health or safety or to infringe on the rights of others. If taking a particular risk may cause harm, don't take the risk.

> *If taking a particular risk*
> *may cause harm, don't take*
> *the risk.*

Second, think twice before deciding to break the rules. Teachers in most schools operate within a set of official or formal policies and procedures. These usually fall under such categories as curriculum standards, discipline protocols, and ordering of supplies.

There are also unofficial practices working within virtually all schools that have as much to do with how a school functions as do the formal ones. These are culture ("This is the way we do things around here") and tradition ("This is the way we've always done them"). In many schools, teachers share such unstated conventions as collectively taking responsibility for all students' learning to write well.

Before you risk doing something new or doing something differently, consider whether taking that risk would violate the formal or informal policies, practices, and perceptions in your school. If so, don't do it. When you gain in experience and have spent a few years in the school, then may be the time to risk working within the system to change policy and procedures and to risk overturning tradition and custom—but as a new teacher, let wisdom and decorum prevail.

SHOULD YOU OR SHOULDN'T YOU?

James Bryant Conant, president of Harvard College from 1933 to 1953, believed in the value of taking risks. "Behold the turtle," he is credited to have said. "It makes progress only when it sticks its neck out."

Suppose you want to "stick your neck out" but are afraid of having your head chopped off? Or suppose you tell someone what you plan to do and he or she responds with a "killer comment" that takes you aback? Some classic—and I would emphatically add *unprofessional*—"killer comments" are

- We tried that before—don't waste your time.
- Get real!
- Where did you dig that one up!
- Been there, done that; didn't work then, won't work now.

Uncertainties and killer comments can give you second thoughts about taking even the most worthwhile risk and can cause you to ask yourself, "What if I take a risk and fail?" Thomas Edison, if you recall, supposedly tried thousands of times before he succeeded in coming up with a filament that made the electric lightbulb possible. "I have not failed," he is purported to have said. "I've just found 10,000 ways that don't work." So ask yourself, "What is the worst thing that can happen if I take the risk and fail?" More than likely, you will decide that informed risks, "while possibly resulting in failures, are worth taking, and that failure is not a catastrophe" (Ellis & Harper, 1961, p. 153).

HELP THE RISK SUCCEED

Once you have decided to take a risk, you may be able to increase its chances of success by doing the following:

1. Define as clearly as possible what you plan to do and why.

2. List everything you can think of that might resist or get in the way of achieving your intended outcome.

3. List everything you can think of that might help achieve your intended outcome.

4. Develop strategies to intensify items that help, dilute items that hinder, and change resisting items into supporting ones.

RISK WITH CONVICTION

Once you have decided to take a risk, do so with confidence and joy. If the risk you consider taking will cause no harm and does not impinge on formal or informal policy and practice, and if you are convinced that taking the risk will reap benefits, then go ahead, take it. After all, as Feiman-Nemser, Schwille, Carver, and Yusko (1999) suggest, "Instead of a culture of politeness, [protégés] need a culture of inquiry. Instead of reliance [on] surface changes and easy answers, [protégés] need an openness

Once you have decided to take a risk, do so with confidence and joy.

to alternative explanations and possibilities and a willingness to experiment and study the results" (p. 20).

What risk have you taken lately that opened up a new and better way to do something or resulted in your learning to teach better? In the left-hand column below, briefly describe what you did and why. In the right-hand column, write what you learned from the experience.

What I Did	*What I Learned*

PRINCIPLES FOR SUCCESS

We all have our own styles and ways of doing things; some work, others don't. Often, it is by trying out new strategies and behaviors that we learn and improve. Changing what we do and how we do it involves risks, including the risk of making things worse and the risk of being ridiculed if things go wrong.

Taking a risk can open up a new learning experience. Before you take a risk, however, consider its potential effect on yourself and others. Once you are certain that it will do no harm and will likely lead to some benefit, don't hold back. Do it the best you can. If possible, get your mentor's support.

Protégés get the most out of being mentored when they are willing to try something new or to try doing something differently in order to learn to teach better. You will be likely to make such risk taking more beneficial and less risky when you do the following:

- Be willing to go "out on a limb," if need be, to follow through on your convictions.
- Resist the impulse to take a risk until you have considered its ramifications.
- Do not take a risk if there is any possibility that doing so will cause harm.
- Once you have decided to take an informed risk, do so with confidence.

CHAPTER EIGHT

Reflect

Everything that happens to you is your teacher. The secret is to learn to sit at the feet of your own life and be taught by it.

Polly B. Berands

When a teacher reflects on her or his professional practice with the objective of learning to teach better, the teacher and learner are the same person. Read the previous sentence again; it has powerful implications. It means that you have the means to mentor yourself and the opportunity to monitor your own professional growth.

> *You have the means to mentor yourself, and the opportunity to monitor your own professional growth.*

One of the best ways to learn from your own experience is through reflection. You can, and probably do, relive many of your experiences in your memory and reflect on them in your thoughts. Chances are, however, that you will learn more from reflection if you do it in writing. Luckner and Nadler (1997) contend that

the act of writing compels the individual to express in symbols specific knowledge originally represented and stored in memory in a different form. . . . Journal writing creates situations that encourage reflection and explicitness, which often leads to a renewed awareness of a person's knowledge. (p. 118)

I asked Cathy Foltz (who for 20 years was a health care worker and is now a new teacher) what she considers one of the best things a new teacher can do to learn to teach better. "Get a journal and write a bit every day," she replied. "Writing helped me clarify my professional problems and successes and provided some documentation of discipline problems. I shared my journal with my mentor so that she could see my daily progress and offer suggestions."

KEEP A PROFESSIONAL LEARNING JOURNAL

Get yourself a notebook, steno pad, or bound journal. In it, write your reflections and discuss them with your mentor. Keeping a journal for learning is not necessarily the same as keeping a diary.

Get yourself a notebook, steno pad, or bound journal. In it, write your reflections and discuss them with your mentor.

There are several ways to structure a professional learning journal, and you can certainly devise your own. In Dumont, New Jersey, for example, new teachers are encouraged to enter lesson plans, examples of student work, and notes from workshops into a portfolio, then write reflections on their portfolio entries.

Another commonly used method is to divide the pages of a notebook into three vertical columns and label them, respectively, (a) "What and Why," (b) "What Happened," and (c) "Reflections." In the first column, succinctly and objectively record what action(s) you did or did not take and why you did or did not take it.

In the second column, indicate what happened as a result of, or in spite of, what was or was not done. Include impressions, feelings, and anecdotes as well as objective data. So far, what you have written is not much different from a diary entry. But don't stop here!

The third column, *Reflections*, is the most important. This is where learning takes place. In the third column, write down why you think things happened the way they did; what you did or did not do that contributed to the outcome—successful or otherwise; and how you might adjust or modify your approach to do it better next time.

When Rosa was a student teacher, she wrote in her three-column journal about her experience assigning homework to a tenth-grade English class. Here is an edited version of what she wrote in the first column:

> The class read *Romeo and Juliet* . . . then briefly discussed it and watched it on film.
>
> The next day, they watched a movie of the musical *West Side Story*, a contemporary version of Shakespeare's story of the star-crossed lovers. I gave the class the following homework assignment: "Describe the dominant traits both Juliet and Maria exhibited concerning their relationship with their family/gang, and give an example of how those traits affected others."
>
> I had hoped the students would see in the musical the traits I wanted them to identify and therefore be better able to understand Juliet's disobedience toward her family. I also expected Tony and Maria's tragedy would help students understand how the trait led to the death of Romeo's cousin.

In the second column of her journal, Rosa described and reacted to the class's response to her assignment. Here are excerpts from that column's entry:

> Out of the class of 25, only 10 students (40%) handed in papers. Of the 10, only 2 wrote about the traits of "disloyalty" and "sacrifice." The others did not even name a trait, nor did they say anything to show they knew what a trait was or that they had an understanding of cause-and-effect relationships. . . . I was frustrated. This was a good class. They generally did their homework and handed in thoughtful papers. . . . Why did they fluff off my assignment? I don't think it's because I'm a student teacher. They listen to me in class and seem engaged for the most part. . . . After I told them the assignment, I asked if there were any questions. No one raised their hand, so I assumed they all understood. . . . When so few papers were

handed in, I asked for an explanation. Most answered, "I didn't understand the assignment."

In the third column, Rosa reflected on what she had written in the first two columns. Most of her frustration centered on her initial supposition that the students understood the assignment. "After all," she wrote, "no one had any questions after I told them what the homework was." Rosa went on to write about how she had sometimes kept quiet in Professor X's class in college when she did not understand something.

> I didn't want to appear stupid or feel uncomfortable asking someone—especially an authority figure—to repeat something just because I didn't get it. . . . Maybe the students didn't understand the meaning of the word *trait*. . . . I should have defined the word for them. Perhaps if I wrote the assignment on the board in addition to giving the assignment verbally, it would have been clearer—especially to the more visual students. . . . How can I be sure whether students understand an assignment? I remember that [my mentor] sometimes, after giving me feedback or telling me about some curriculum issue, would ask me to repeat back in my own words what I understood her to have said—"Rogerian listening," I think she called it. It did help my understanding. Next time we meet, I will ask [my mentor] whether she thinks using Rogerian listening and writing the assignment on the board will help students' understanding.

In the three-column format below, reflect on something you recently did.

What and Why	What Happened	Reflections

GUIDED REFLECTION

Hole and McEntee (1999) have developed protocols, or guidelines, to enable teachers to reflect alone or with colleagues. Their Guided Reflection Protocol for individual reflection follows the five steps summarized below.

1. *Collect stories.* Keep a set of index cards or a steno book close at hand for that purpose.

2. *What happened?* Choose and write succinctly a story that strikes you as particularly interesting.

3. *Why did it happen?* Answer the question in a way that makes sense to you.

4. *What might it mean?* Explore several possible meanings rather than trying to write the "correct" one.

5. *What are the implications for practice?* On the basis of under-standings from the earlier steps, consider how your practice might change.

Some practitioners believe that collaborative reflection can have a greater impact than solitary reflection simply because others can "push" you to look deeper and harder—to go to places you may not think about or even be willing to think about. In addition to their protocol for individual reflection, Hole and McEntee (1999) have also developed guidelines that allow teachers to collaborate, to share stories about their professional experiences in ways that can be learning opportunities for both the individuals and the group. Their Critical Incidents Protocol for shared reflection follows the seven steps summarized below:

1. *Write stories.* Each group member writes a description of what happened. (10 minutes)

2. *Choose a story.* The group decides which story to use. (5 minutes)

3. *What happened?* The selected story is read by the presenter and set within the context of professional goals. (10 minutes)

4. *Why did it happen?* Colleagues ask clarifying questions. (5 minutes)

5. *What might it mean?* The incident is discussed in the context of the presenter's work; the presenter listens. (15 minutes)

6. *What are the implications for practice?* The presenter responds, and the group engages in conversation about implications for their own and the presenter's practice. (15 minutes)

7. *Debrief the process.* The group discusses what just happened and how the process worked. (10 minutes)

FOCUSED REFLECTION

Reflection that focuses on teaching and learning can hasten a new teacher's development as a self-reliant teacher. A self-reliant teacher is one who is willing and able to (a) generate and choose purposefully from among viable alternatives, (b) act upon those choices, (c) monitor and reflect upon the consequences of applying those choices, and (d) modify and adjust in order to enhance student learning.

> *Reflection that focuses on teaching and learning can hasten a new teacher's development as a self-reliant teacher.*

Margaret M., a mentor-teacher in California's Beginning Teacher Support and Assessment program (BTSA), reports that her protégés—whose focus is to gather evidence from students, reflect on those data, and modify practice accordingly—move ahead much more rapidly than those who do not focus and reflect. On the basis of her experience, Margaret offers the following advice and observations about focused reflection:

- The basis for reflection must be student work—objective evidence. Otherwise, reflections are based on perceptions that are not always accurate.
- Novices tend to confine reflections to impressions and feelings. New teachers should reflect under the guidance and structure of a veteran teacher. If they are prompted by

"hard" questions, new teachers will quickly become skilled in the process.

- Reflection can be built into your day. You can even do it while commuting. Always ask yourself the big questions:

What did my students do well today?

What did I do to facilitate their learning?

What did my students have difficulty with today?

What could I have done to prevent that difficulty or to correct it once it surfaced?

PRINCIPLES FOR SUCCESS

You can help your mentor help you by paying attention to the things that you did or did not do, why you did or didn't do them, and what happened as a result; contemplating how you can use the experience to improve; and discussing your reflections with your mentor.

Protégés get the most out of being mentored when they pay attention to their professional experiences, critically examine the implications of those experiences, and reflect on their reflections with input from their mentor or colleagues. You will be likely to get the most out of reflecting on professional experiences when you do the following:

- Be clear about *why* you make particular decisions.
- Pay attention to the results of your decision making.
- Analyze your actions, motivations, and outcomes in order to learn to teach better.
- Write your reflections down.
- Share and discuss your reflections with your mentor.
- Revise your practice based on what you have learned from your own reflections and your mentor's feedback.

CHAPTER NINE

Give Back

Ask not what your country can do for you—ask what you can do for your country.

John F. Kennedy

The previous chapters have focused on what you, the protégé, can do to help the mentoring process help you. This chapter deals with the flip side of the coin—what opportunities you might have to give something back to the mentoring program and to take a hand in reshaping the school's culture and philosophy.

LEAVE A LEGACY

A responsibility of every teacher is to contribute somehow to the profession. Teachers new to a school are uniquely equipped to address that responsibility because they bring with them new ideas, new knowledge, and new energy. Let's look first at how you, as a new teacher, can contribute to the betterment of your school's mentoring program.

Teachers new to a school are uniquely equipped because they bring with them new ideas, new knowledge, and new energy.

You can play an important role in improving your school's mentoring program by assisting in the program's evaluation and revision efforts. In many districts, mentoring coordinators

58

conduct surveys, structure interviews, carry out observations, or in some other way gather feedback from teachers who are in their first year or have just completed their first year of teaching. An analysis of this kind of data has often led to significant improvements. For example, in one district, mentors were filing reports with principals about their meetings with protégés. Because of this, the new teachers suspected that mentors were participating in the teachers' formal evaluations, so they were reluctant to divulge to their mentors any problems they might be having in the classroom. The situation resolved itself when the new teachers realized that only meeting times and dates were being reported, not the content of the discussions. It became clear that the reports were solely for purposes of accountability because mentors received stipends.

If you are asked for feedback about the program, give it conscientiously, thoroughly, and honestly. If your mentoring program does not elicit input from new teachers in order to help assess and improve the mentoring program, consider being proactive: Offer your suggestions, and even your assistance.

> *If you are asked for feedback about the program, give it conscientiously, thoroughly, and honestly.*

Sometimes, mentors will ask new teachers for help. Resource C, "Chatboard Exchange on the Internet," shows a request for help posted on the Internet by a mentor-teacher and the set of responses she received from new teachers.

BE A CHANGE AGENT

Years ago, when I was a beginning teacher, Mike Massailo took it upon himself to be my mentor. Mike was an experienced teacher in the school where we both taught. He was highly respected and very savvy about the inner workings of the system. "This school has a culture," he told me, "and that culture is strong. You may or may not like it, but you need to go along with it. On the basis of a few of our conversations, you have some good ideas that will really benefit students. But new ways of doing things won't fly around here until there is more flexibility in some areas and more structure in others."

Mike went on to tell me that most of the veteran teachers and administrators—"the old guard," he called them—realized that such changes were needed, but they had more or less acclimated themselves to the status quo.

"Well," I said, "I haven't been around here long enough to have become acclimated. Perhaps I can do something to help it happen."

"Perhaps you can," said Mike. "You are young, intelligent, and enthusiastic. A word of advice, however. Wait until you have taught here for at least 1 or 2 years before you try to change anything."

I took Mike's advice, and by the end of my second year, in collaboration with two other teachers and with Mike's behind-the-scenes counsel, I did succeed in changing some student discipline policies (for the better, I was told) and injecting more professionally oriented discussion into the teachers' room conversations.

Can you be a change agent? Toward the end of your first full year of teaching, gather together a group of colleagues to discuss and answer the following questions:

1. What, if anything, can be done differently in our school that would result in students learning better, teachers teaching better, and/or supplies and materials being used more effectively?

_____

_____

_____

2. How might those changes be made?

_____

_____

_____

Here are some ways to help change happen (Portner, 1998, p. 69):

1. Define the desired change, using specific, measurable terms.

2. List everything you can think of that is resisting or getting in the way of that change.

3. List everything you can think of that is helping or can help that change take place.

4. Develop strategies to intensify items that help, dilute items that hinder, and change resisting items into supporting ones.

EXPERIENCED NEWCOMERS

Are you an experienced teacher who has become a "newcomer" again because you have changed schools or even districts? Or perhaps you are a novice in the classroom but have spent years in another profession. Gary Hartzell (1990) suggests that experienced newcomers can immediately contribute to their new school by "involving themselves in important activities outside their immediate job description" (p. 30). He encourages experienced newcomers to sit on committees and to assume responsibility for projects that draw upon their expertise.

Ken R. is an experienced newcomer. Ken spent 12 years as a copywriter and account executive in a midsized advertising company before going back to school and changing careers. Ken is now a first-year teacher in a large high school. He assists the advisor to the school newspaper and has volunteered to be on the school's community outreach committee.

THE GIFT OF RENEWAL

Robert Fulghum (1991) reminds us what happens when we ask a kindergarten class, "How many of you can draw?" "All hands shoot up. Yes, of course we can draw—all of us. What can you draw? Anything! . . . How many of you can sing? All hands. . . . Let's sing! Now? Why not! . . . Try these same questions on a college (or older) audience. . . . You can imagine the response . . . What went wrong between kindergarten and college? What happened to YES! of course I can" (pp. 238-239)?

Yes! of course I can—*and so can you!* Such confidence and exuberance are perhaps the greatest gifts a beginning teacher can bring to her or his new colleagues. Sure, as a novice, you probably have a lot to learn before you acquire the skills

Confidence and exuberance are perhaps the greatest gifts a beginning teacher can bring to her or his new colleagues.

and understandings of your experienced associates. You may envy the nonchalant ease with which they handle even the most harrowing situation, and you may even marvel at their uncanny ability to manage their classrooms. But if you are excited about teaching, are enthusiastic about the prospect of learning to teach better, and are able to convey your confidence and exuberance to others, you can literally revitalize a school and its teachers.

Finally, when you have become an experienced, self-reliant teacher, it will be time to remember and repay the help and support you received when you were a beginner and to become a mentor yourself to a new teacher!

PRINCIPLES FOR SUCCESS

As a "new kid on the block," you bring a new set of eyes, a new perspective, and new energy to a school. You have the ability to contribute to the mentoring program's development, to improvement in the way your school operates, and perhaps even to the revitalization of some burned-out teachers.

Protégés get the most out of being mentored when they are able and willing to give something back in return. You will be contributing to the operation, culture, and overall improvement of your mentoring program and school when you do the following:

- Provide relevant feedback that assists in the mentoring program's evaluation and revision efforts.
- Actively seek out opportunities to help with projects or programs that would result in students learning better, teachers teaching better, and supplies and materials being used more effectively.
- Look for opportunities to share and use your past experience to help students, other teachers, and your school.
- Share your enthusiasm for teaching and learning with your more experienced colleagues.

R E S O U R C E A

Internet Sites
and Publications
for New Teachers

Here is a compilation of some of the electronic and printed resources that new and prospective educators may find helpful as they navigate the unfamiliar pathway stretching from preinduction through the first few years of teaching. There are more materials out there, of course, and more become available almost daily. The resources listed below are ones recommended by those currently on the journey.

ON THE INTERNET

Internet education chatboards form, disband, and sometimes re-form over time as dictated by the needs of their participants. The following sites are actively on-line as of this writing.

www.coreknowledge.org
Lesson plans and other goodies from the E. D. Hirsh Core Knowledge program.

http://homepages.luc.edu/~hweiman/page3ed.html
An extensive set of links to a variety of K-12 and college education Web sites.

www.coollessons.org/coolunits.htm
For K-12 teachers, a rich source of ready-made units and lessons for most subjects, this site also helps teachers design their

own units. Included are technology-engaged learning models such as WebQuests, Research Modules, and Problem-Based-Learning.

www.lessonplanspage.com
Lesson plans developed by teachers for teachers. Plans are accessible for just about any subject and grade level.

www.sitesforteachers.com
A comprehensive listing of clickable links to a wide array of sites for teachers.

http://edweek.org/ew/events/calendar.htm
An interactive search-by-month site for regional and national education conferences and other events.

http://inspiringteachers.com/mentoring/index.html
"Ask a Mentor" and "New Teacher Message Board" are only two of several networking features of this beginning teacher tool kit.

http://teachers.net
A rich collection of topic-specific chatboards, articles, and materials covering just about every aspect of K-12 education.

www.education-world.com/a_admin/admin139/html
Links to on-line opportunities for teacher networking and special interest groups.

www.tappedin.org
An interactive on-line community of educators engaged in professional development programs and informal collaborative educational activities.

http://home.talkcity.com/libraryDr/edupeople/
Brings teachers, students, and parents together in real-time scheduled chats and topical conferences. Offers teaching tips and lesson plans. A Spanish chat section is one of its features.

BOOKS AND ARTICLES

Appleman, D., & McClear, J. (1998). *Teacher, the children are here: A guide for teachers of the elementary grades.* Glenview, IL: Scott, Foresman. A step-by-step guide taking the teacher from the week before school starts through to the following summer, with suggested strategies to use along the way.

Archer, J. (2001). First impressions. *Education Week*, *21*(1), 48-54. To relate some of how it feels to be a first-year teacher, *Education Week* tracked five novice middle school educators from September 2000 through June 2001. This article reports a few of their ups and downs and some of what they learned about teaching.

Callahan, J. F., Clark, L. H., & Kellough, R. D. (1997). *Teaching in the middle and secondary schools* (6th ed.). Upper Saddle River, NJ: Merrill/Prentice Hall. How to plan and carry out instruction—presented in a modular format.

Canter, L., & Canter, M. (1999). *First class teacher: Success strategies for new teachers*. Santa Monica, CA: Lee Canter & Associates. Strategies, lesson ideas, activities, and reproducibles for teachers, parents, and students.

DePaul, A. (1998). *What to expect your first year of teaching*. Washington, DC: U.S. Department of Education, Office of Educational Research and Improvement. The author asked a group of award-winning teachers who had just completed their first year on the job to describe their challenges and to offer advice for overcoming obstacles. This book presents and summarizes their comments, lists resources, and offers tips for first-year teachers.

DePaul, A. (2000). *Survival guide for new teachers*. Washington, DC: U.S. Department of Education, Office of Educational Research and Improvement. The author quotes and comments on the thoughts of award-winning teachers who have just completed their first year on the job.

Donaldson, M. L., & Poon, B. (Eds.). (1999). *Reflections of first-year teachers on school culture: Questions, hope, and challenges*. San Francisco: Jossey-Bass. This book's eight chapters present the experience of eight beginning teachers through personal reflection, presentation of individual cases, and analysis of challenges and supports.

Fogarty, R. (2001). *Ten things new teachers need to succeed*. Arlington Heights, IL: Skylight Professional Development. A quick reference (a "slice of life in the world of the teacher" as the author puts it), this 38-page publication presents a sampling of the demands of teaching. The 10 concise chapters make good discussion starters on such topics as seeking a mentor, the classroom environment, making decisions on the run, student discipline, curriculum standards, curriculum core content, planning lessons, instructional strategies, student assessment, and involving parents.

Jonson, K. (1997). *The new elementary teacher's handbook.* Thousand Oaks, CA: Corwin. This 224-page workbook provides practical suggestions for many of the concerns facing a new teacher, such as maintaining discipline, organizing time and the classroom, and student assessment.

Kottler, E., & Kottler, J. (1998). *Secrets for secondary school teachers: How to succeed in your first year.* Thousand Oaks, CA: Corwin. Tips and strategies from experienced teachers to organize the workload and reduce stress.

Moran, C., Stobbe, J., Baron, W., Miller, J., & Moir, E. (2000). *Keys to the classroom: A teacher guide for the first month of school* (2nd ed.). Thousand Oaks, CA: Corwin. A guide to such issues as setting the learning environment and establishing daily routines. Also offered are lesson plans, classroom management strategies, and special aids for teaching bilingual students, including sample songs and letters to parents in English and Spanish.

Orange, C. (2000). *25 biggest mistakes teachers make and how to avoid them.* Thousand Oaks, CA: Corwin. Almost every beginning teacher makes mistakes—uninformed strategies, impulsive discipline, inadvertent slights, inappropriate remarks in jest. This book presents over 300 scenarios accompanied by prescriptions for appropriate handling of such potential errors.

Parkway, F. W., & Stanford, B. (2000). *Becoming a teacher* (5th ed.). Boston: Allyn & Bacon. Case studies and discussion of teacher leadership, mentoring, classroom dynamics, on-line activities for professional development, and developing a professional portfolio.

Pierangelo, R. (1996). *A survival kit for the special education teacher.* West Nyack, NY: Center for Applied Research in Education. Methods for clinical and case study and a discussion of the responsibilities and roles of the special education teacher.

Recruiting New Teachers. (1998). *Take this job and love it! Making the mid-career move to teaching.* Boston: Author. A reference of information compiled for those contemplating switching careers to become a teacher. The book briefly discusses teaching in schools today and how to get certified, but the bulk of the book is a detailed, state-by-state listing of teacher education programs that offer services to "older" students.

Recruiting New Teachers. (2000). *How to become a teacher: A complete guide*. Boston: Author. A resource for those seeking information about financial aid, on-line job banks, profiles of teachers, information about teacher preparation programs, licensure, and how to decide if teaching is right for them.

Rosenblum-Lowden, R. (2000). *You have to go to school . . . you're the teacher!* (2nd ed.). Thousand Oaks, CA: Corwin. Contains 250 tips and classroom management strategies to establish student responsibility, set routines and consequences, and work with parents.

Strohmer, J. C. (1997). *Time-saving tips for teachers*. Thousand Oaks, CA: Corwin. This publication is targeted at teachers who need to become more efficient in their use of time for communicating, planning, assessing, etc. It contains over 50 reproducible forms to use for a variety of situations.

Wong, H. K., & Wong, R. T. (1998). *The first days of school: How to be an effective teacher* (2nd ed.). Mountain View, CA: Harry K. Wong Publications, Inc. Twenty-six chapters offering clear and pertinent understandings and how-to tips about such nitty-gritty concerns as effective teaching, high expectations, enhancing student behavior and learning, classroom management, taking roll, maintaining a grade book, designing lessons, and building student achievement.

Resource B

Professional Education Organizations and Their Web Pages

American Association of School Librarians
www.ala.org/aasl

American Council on the Teaching of Foreign Languages
www.actfl.org

American Federation of Teachers
www.aft.org

Association for Career and Technical Education
www.avaonline.org

Council for Exceptional Children
www.cec.sped.org

International Technology Education Association
www.iteawww.org

National Art Education Association
www.naea-reston.org

National Association for Music Education
www.menc.org

National Association for Bilingual Education
www.nabe.org

National Association for Sport and Physical Education
www.aahperd.org/naspe/naspe_main.html

National Board for Professional Teaching Standards
www.nbpts.org/standards/

National Center for Health Education
www.nche.org/new2001

National Council for the Social Studies
www.socialstudies.org

National Council of Teachers of English
www.ncte.org

National Council of Teachers of Mathematics
www.nctm.org

National Education Association
www.nea.org

National Science Teachers Association
http://nsta.org

Chatboard Exchange on the Internet

Following is a slightly edited set of actual postings on the Beginning Teachers Chatboard (http://teachers.net).

Posted by Kristi on 8/31/01:

I am mentoring a new teacher. I would like some opinions out there from other new teachers and other teachers who have mentored. The new teacher, let's call her S, was hired and my principal LOVED her. I feel like I am totally overwhelming her with information. But, it is all things she does need to know. She is very quiet and maybe shy. She hasn't said a word, asked a question, she just nods. S is a very sweet person. But, I feel like I have to teach her how to teach. I am getting the feeling that she is very unsure of herself, or just didn't have a good student teaching experience. She doesn't talk. I don't want to make her feel bad, so I am asking you, new teachers, how do you suggest I handle this? Would you like your mentor to continue to talk about this and that or should I back off? Do you think she is shy or I am telling too much—is that possible? Or is she just taking it all in?

Here is some of what I did, would this be too much for you? I sat down and went over our schedule. I made a booklet for her with notes about each subject area and things we do in our school. How we handle things, our procedures. . . . I photocopied information from books to help her. As I told her, I think me talking is one thing but by making up this folder, she can sit down and digest it all on her own time. Then she can ask all the questions she wants since we have all "been there." As I told her no question is stupid—we all had a million or two!

71

I gave her a tour and introduced her to everyone she will be working with. I helped her to arrange her room. I gave her my first 2 weeks of plans so she has something to work with. I even copied my files for a few Big Books she can use this month. I copied my beginning of school file as well as my open house notes. I copied my poetry notebook too. I think I am going out of my way and she doesn't talk, ask questions, or even say thanks. I know she has great qualities but she is so timid, I think.

Let me add that I did not do all this in one day. Last spring, after she was hired, I had her come in and observe me and a Kindergarten class for the day and then met with her a little at a time this summer. I even made a little package up with stickers and notepads to say WELCOME!

Any suggestions how I can help her to open up? I really want S to be prepared and I want to help her out. And, I want her to be happy on our team. . . . Thanks for your insight!

Posted by Jenna on 8/31/01:
I am a first year teacher and ADORE my mentor teacher for all she has done. . . . It really helps. . . . I appreciated it SOOOO much. . . . What would I do without the info??? I have NO IDEA.

I think what you're doing is AWESOME. . . . Perhaps "S" is just shy or does not like this help . . . who knows why. Just lay low from here on in and just check in with her. . . . If she wants or needs the help . . . she'll ask. . . . She already has the feeling you will contribute whatever she needs.

Posted by Tammy on 8/31/01:
You sound like you are doing a great job as a mentor. I loved my mentor but he missed telling me the basics, like how to do attendance.

As far as "S" is concerned, she sounds a lot like me. I am very quiet and shy until I get to know the people and the situation. But while I am being quiet, I'm listening to everything that goes on. If someone comments that I don't talk much, I may tell them it's because I don't have anything important to say yet. When I do they will know. I also have no problem getting up and talking to a class full of kids, but a room full of adults or even just meeting a new person still sometimes gives me the shakes. I think "S" will do fine as long as you continue to make yourself available to her.

Posted by Susanna on 8/31/01:

Kristi, you are being wonderfully generous and I know how much those with experience want to make sure that people new to the profession learn from mistakes made in the past. Think about your own students, however. As much as you want to provide them with a rich, fulfilling experience, some just need more time to take it all in. S could be "slow to warm up." She could be completely overwhelmed by the enormity of the task that she has undertaken. She might also want to make her own way. Have you seen her teach yet? Allow her to be the professional she is. Give her some breathing room. Keep checking in. Maybe set up a regular time to meet so that she can gather her questions.

This teaching thing is massive. As a first-year teacher (who doesn't start until 9/6), I'm feeling like hiding my head under the sand right about now. I needed a solid two weeks to set up my physical classroom space before I could meet with my grade partner and get the information that would be most useful to me. You are being super caring and supportive. I'm sure that S appreciates it; she might not have the energy to express it yet! Good luck!

Posted by Lisa on 8/31/01:

I'm a new teacher. I've been one for about 3 weeks, and I was a lot like your mentee at first! Don't be put off because she's so quiet. During my orientations and everything else I rarely asked questions. Everything was so new and so much to digest that I needed to take time to let things sink in, really look at everything, and make sure I knew what I understood and didn't. People kept asking me if I had questions, and I always told them that I'd let them know when I got to that point! That's one reason she's probably so quiet.

I have other theories, all of which applied to me at first! First of all, she may be intimidated by you because you know everything. Even though she's been told that no question is stupid, she might still think that some of her concerns are either trivial or things that she feels like she should know by now. Until she gets to know you better, she may be hesitant to approach you unless it's something important.

On a different note, she may be very independent and wants to do things for herself. That feeling of getting your first classroom is incredible. You can finally arrange and decorate your own space. You can make your own rules, rewards, and consequences.

You can plan lessons the way you want to without a supervisor constantly monitoring everything. She probably has tons of ideas that she wants to try out. She may just want to try everything out and see how things go.

On a related note, she may also be concerned with wanting to appear professional and not a rookie. I know of first year teachers who have basically done exactly what their mentor did. I could never do that, because I feel like I am a teacher now, I have earned my classroom, and I want to show everyone what I am capable of. I don't want to be looked down on because I'm new. She may feel the same way. Please don't take it personal that she hasn't asked questions or really talked. If she's shy by nature, and is going through any of the above, it's no surprise she's acting this way! You've given her so much help and sound like a great mentor. Let her take everything in. I'm sure that she'll come to you when she's ready!!

Posted by Kristina on 8/31/01:
My suggestion would be to keep plugging away. Ask her to join you for lunch or join the weekend happy hour. In about a month, she'll have internalized everything and will probably need your help with planning. Maybe you can set up one night a week to plan with her. My mentor did that with me, and it was very helpful. Keep up the great work and have a terrific year!

Posted by Christine on 8/31/01:
You sound fabulous. My school district had so many new teachers and so few mentors that I didn't get one. You seem to have done all that you can to get "S" prepared for the start of school. Why don't you give her two school weeks to take the info. that you have given her and apply it. Maybe by then she will feel more comfortable with the staff and she'll have more questions to ask because she will then have her feet wet. I am very friendly but when I am in a new situation I am very quiet, also. Another suggestion is to give her your email address. It is sometimes easier to type then to ask questions face to face.

Posted by Second Year Teacher on 9/01/01:
When I first started I didn't ask many questions either. I was just smiling and nodding (or trembling and nodding, depending on the situation. . .). I had so many I didn't know where to start! And many of them weren't things I really needed to know from

day one. It almost didn't seem possible to pick out a couple of questions and ask them when I really had questions about EVERYTHING. Besides, I knew I could get through a few days without asking the questions. Later when I had a little experience, I started asking my questions.

As for giving her so much information, if it is all things she needs to know, don't worry about it being too much information. She may not remember all of it but it sounds like you have made it clear she shouldn't feel bad about having to come back and ask you to repeat some of it. However, if you are telling her things that you KNOW she won't need to know for a while, it might be better to wait until the "need-to-know-this-right-now!" stuff has sunk in.

By the way I absolutely agree with another post that said being shy around adults is not the same as being shy in front of students. I am the same way. Unfortunately that sometimes meant I would do fine as long as I was the only adult in my classroom, but as soon as I was being observed, I would get nervous and shy. Ironically I would get the most nervous when I was observed by people I knew well—I guess because their approval meant more to me. Although finding such a person should not be your role, it might help "S" to find a second person she can talk to that ISN'T her mentor, so that she can ask them things she may not have understood when you explained them, maybe they could see her teaching sometime and give her different feedback than you would.

Posted by Christine W. on 9/01/01:

I agree with many of the above posters! I am a new teacher this year and it seems like there is a never-ending supply of techniques and procedures to learn, along with meeting many new people and getting a feel for the political ground.

I know that I may appear to be much like your mentee! It is very overwhelming to learn everything so quickly and there is too much to digest to even begin forming questions. I think it would be a good idea to let your mentee have some time to begin formulating her thoughts and to start doing things her way before more is thrown at her. One of my advisors says that some people need to see the big picture before they can learn the details. . . . Perhaps you mentee needs to get the year started before addressing every little aspect of the school environment.

Finally, please be aware that this person may want to discover things on her own and begin gaining independence. You sound like a wonderful mentor, but it may be difficult to have everything handed to you like that. . . . I would feel like my mother were there watching over every move I made. I like to learn things on my own and ask questions as I have them. I might feel a bit smothered and bothered by that fact that I would not have the chance to "sink-or-swim" because I love to test my own abilities.

I think that you should ask the mentee if she would like help with anything or if she needs anything else. If she says "No" or "Not right now," I would see that as a big hint that she is ready to be more independent and to use you as a resource.

References

Carr, J., Herman, N., & Harris, D. (2001, March). *Colleague consultation: A continuum for collaborative renewal.* Paper presented at the national conference of the Association of Supervision and Curriculum Development, Boston.

Champion, R. (2001). Planning for action, step by step. *Journal of Staff Development, 22*(4), 62-63.

Collins, J. J. (1992). *Developing writing and thinking skills across the curriculum: A practical program for schools.* Rowley, MA: Author. Available from The Network Inc., 136 Fenno Drive, Rowley, MA 01969-1004, phone 800-877-5400, www.thenetworkinc.org

DePaul, A. (1998). *What to expect your first year of teaching.* Washington, DC: U.S. Department of Education, Office of Educational Research and Improvement.

DePaul, A. (2000). *Survival guide for new teachers.* Washington, DC: U.S. Department of Education, Office of Educational Research and Improvement. Retrieved September 5, 2001, from www.ed.pubs/survivalguide/message.html

Ellis, A., & Harper, R. (1961). *A guide to rational living.* Englewood Cliffs, NJ: Prentice Hall.

Feiman-Nemser, S., Schwille, S., Carver, C., & Yusko, B. (1999). *A conceptual review of literature on new teacher induction.* College Park, MD: National Partnership for Excellence and Accountability in Teaching.

Fulghum, R. (1991). *Uh-oh.* New York: Villard.

Gazda, G. M., Asbury, F., Balzer, F. J., Childers, W. C., & Walters, R. P. (1991). *Human relations development: A manual for educators* (4th ed.). Boston: Allyn & Bacon.

Hartzell, G. N. (1990). Introduction of experienced teachers into a new school site. *Journal of Staff Development, 11*(4), 28-31.

Hole, S., & McEntee, G. H. (1999). Reflection is at the heart of practice. *Educational Leadership, 56*(8), 34-37.

Jakubowski-Spector, P. (1973). Facilitating the growth of women through assertive training. *Counseling Psychologist, 4*(1), 75-86.

Keller, J. (2001). Success myths. *Attitude Is Everything, 11*(3), 3.

Luckner, J. L., & Nadler, R. S. (1997). *Processing the experience: Strategies to enhance and generalize learning* (2nd ed.). Dubuque, IA: Kendall/Hunt.

National Commission on Teaching and America's Future. (1996, September). *What matters most: Teaching for America's future.* New York: Columbia University, Teachers College.

Portner, H. (1998). *Mentoring new teachers.* Thousand Oaks, CA: Corwin.

Scherer, M. (2001). Improving the quality of the teaching force: A conversation with David C. Berliner. *Educational Leadership, 58*(8), 6-11.

Scholtes, P. (1988). *The team handbook.* Madison, WI: Joiner Associates Inc.

Wildman, T., Niles, J., Magliaro, S., & McLaughlin, R. (1989). Teaching and learning to teach: The two roles of beginning teachers. *Elementary School Journal, 89*, 471-492.

Wong, H. K. (2001). Mentoring can't do it all. *Education Week, 20*(43), 46-50.

**CORWIN
PRESS**

The Corwin Press logo—a raven striding across an open book—represents the happy union of courage and learning. We are a professional-level publisher of books and journals for K-12 educators, and we are committed to creating and providing resources that embody these qualities. Corwin's motto is "Success for All Learners."